Collins Illustrated

KOREA

Daniel P. Reid

Photography by Alain Evrard

COLLINS

8 Grafton Street, London W1
1988

William Collins Sons & Co. Ltd
London • Glasgow • Sydney • Auckland
Toronto • Johannesburg

British Library Cataloguing in Publication Data

Collins Illustrated Guide to Korea — (Asian Guides Series)
1. Korea — Description and Travel — Guide books
I. Series
915.92′0448   DS805.2

ISBN 0-00-217952-0

First published 1988
© The Guidebook Company Ltd 1988

Editors: David Price and Martin Williams
Picture Editor: Ingrid Morejohn

Photography by Alain Evrard-Globe Press with additional contributions by
Lyle Lawson (10−11, 113, 130−1)

Maps designed by Bai Yiliang
Design and artwork by Li Design Associates

Printed in Hong Kong

Contents

Young woman courier wearing Olympics cap.

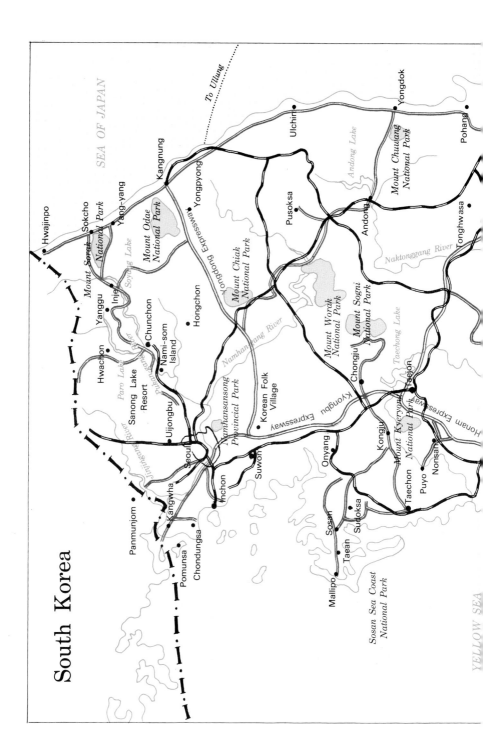

South Korea

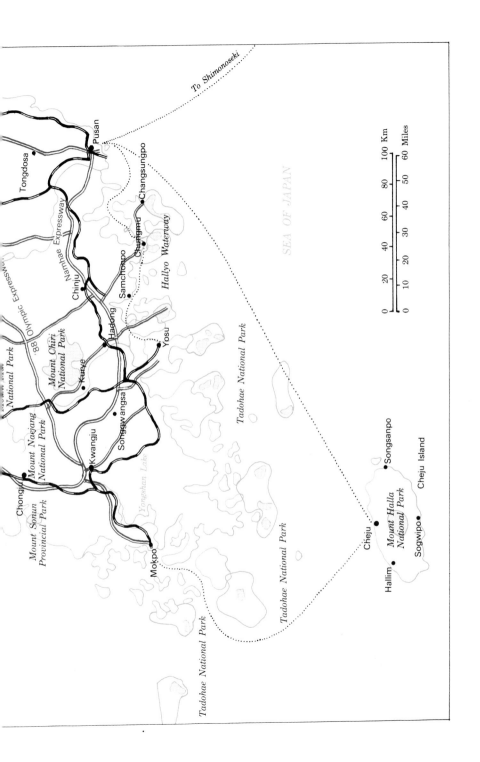

The Land of Morning Calm

The ancient Chinese, who regarded Korea as a friendly tributary state and an honourable younger brother, called it 'Chosun', the 'Land of Morning Calm'. Korean kings, like Chinese emperors, took the dragon as their symbol of divine authority, but in order to keep the relationship between the two thrones clear, the royal Korean dragon was depicted with four claws, while the imperial Chinese dragon bore five.

The Mongols rode roughshod across the Korean peninsula, reducing it to a vast pasture for their horses and cattle during their attempt to conquer Japan via Korea in the 14th century. Two hundred years later Manchu cavalry arrived in force and overran Korea in their campaign to topple China's Ming Dynasty.

The Japanese referred to Koreans as 'the garlic eaters', made repeated attempts to conquer their country and eradicate their culture, and imposed 36 years of brutal colonial rule on Korea from 1910 to 1945.

Less than 40 years ago Korea again became a battleground as the communist and free worlds fought it out in one of history's bloodiest wars, and once again Korea was reduced to ruins.

Korean history has been anything but calm. 'When whales fight, the shrimp gets hurt,' states an old Korean saying. It is small wonder that Korea became disenchanted with foreigners and slammed shut its gates to the outside world, thereby earning itself the name 'Hermit Kingdom'.

Korea's civilization is almost as old as China's and much older than Japan's. And while Korea has historically served as a bridge between China and Japan and shares certain ancient traditions with both, Korean culture has moulded those traditions in very different ways.

Today, 'Hermit Kingdom' is a more appropriate name for communist North Korea, which has been sealed from the outside world since the Korean War. South Korea, by contrast, has become an active member of the world community, an enthusiastic participant in international sports and other events, and a successful trading partner with the world's most economically advanced nations.

Juxtaposed with the background of Korea's elegant temple roofs and scenic landscapes are the incongruous outlines of modern factories, power lines and high-rise construction. But for Koreans, these contrasts pose no contradictions. The old and new balance one another, providing a harmonious blend of the modern and traditional which satisfies both the spiritual and economic needs of the people.

Getting to Korea

By Air

Fourteen international airlines operate over 200 flights weekly to and from Korea. Korean Air, Japan Airlines, Northwest Orient and United Airlines connect Seoul with Los Angeles, San Francisco, Honolulu, New York and Chicago. Other airlines connect Seoul with Tokyo, Taipei, Hong Kong, Singapore and other Asian destinations. A stop in Seoul is often included in round-the-world and regional airline tickets at no extra charge.

Entry to Korea is possible through three international airports: Kimpo International Airport, 17 kilometres (10.5 miles) west of Seoul; Kimhae International Airport, 27 kilometres (17 miles) northwest of Pusan and Cheju International Airport, four kilometres (2.5 miles) west of Cheju City on Cheju Island.

By Sea

Pusan, Korea's second largest city and principal port, is the only international gateway by sea to Korea. Many international cruise ships make a stop at Pusan, which is also the terminus of scheduled ferry services between Japan and Korea. The Pukwan Ferry operates three times a week between the Japanese port of Shimonoseki and Pusan, and the Kukche Ferry links Osaka and Pusan with a twice-weekly service.

Information for Travellers

Visas

Unless exempt, all foreign visitors to Korea who wish to stay longer than 15 days must first obtain a valid visa from a Korean consulate or embassy overseas. Visitors who arrive with confirmed outbound tickets may stay up to 15 days without a visa.
There are two types of visa for Korea:
Short-term Valid for up to 90 days.
Long-term For those wishing to stay in Korea for more than 90 days; requires an entry permit from the Ministry of Justice. Long-term visa holders are also required to apply for a residence certificate at a local district immigration office in Korea.
Visa exemption agreements exist between Korea and the following countries:
For stays not exceeding 90 days: Austria, Bangladesh, Chile, Colombia, Costa Rica, Dominican Republic, Greece, Liberia, Liechtenstein, Malaysia, Mexico, Pakistan, Peru, Singapore, Switzerland and Thailand.
For stays not exceeding 60 days: Belgium, Denmark, Finland, Germany, Iceland, Italy, Lesotho, Luxemburg, Netherlands, Norway, Portugal, Spain, Surinam, Sweden, Turkey and the United Kingdom.
For stays not exceeding 30 days: France and Tunisia.

Customs

You must make a written customs declaration for all valuables and unaccompanied baggage upon entering Korea, but oral declarations generally suffice for hand baggage and personal effects.
You may bring the following items into Korea without paying any duty: two bottles of liquor (up to 760 cc each); 400 cigarettes, 50 cigars, 250 grams (8.75 ounces) of pipe tobacco and 100 grams (3.5 ounces) of other tobacco (total weight of tobacco not to exceed 500 grams or 17.5 ounces); personal effects such as clothing and toiletries; 60 grams (two ounces) of perfume and gifts up to a value of W100,000 (US$122).
Approval is required from the Ministry of Culture and Information in order to take out Korean antiques and valuable cultural artefacts. This may be obtained from the Cultural Properties Maintenance Office, tel. (02) 737−3655 in Seoul, or from its office at Kimpo Airport, tel. (02) 662−0196.

Climate and Clothing

Korea has a temperate climate with four distinct seasons. The peninsula is subjected both to cold, northwesterly winds from Siberia and Manchuria and to warm, monsoon winds from the south Pacific basin.

Spring The annual spring thaw commences in April and the season lasts for two months, until mid-June. Average temperatures hover between 10° and 16°C (50° and 56°F) in Seoul. Spring weather is generally sunny and clear, with occasional drizzle. Lightweight, casual clothes for daytime, with a few thin sweaters and jackets for cool evenings and chilly mountain air, are appropriate clothing for spring.

Summer The summer season stretches from mid-June until mid-September and is characterized by hot, humid weather, with occasional thunder-showers during July and August. Temperatures range from 18–24°C (65–75°F) in the northern parts of the peninsula, and 24–30°C (75–85°F) in the southern portions. Summer clothing should include light cotton shirts, loose-fitting comfortable trousers, swimming attire and other sportswear, and some form of light rain-gear.

Autumn Autumn is by far the best time of year to travel in Korea. Not only is the climate most comfortable then, the air is also at its clearest, and the foliage flames with bright shades of red and gold. The season lasts from mid-September until mid-November, when average temperatures range between 12° and 18°C (55° and 65°F). Lightweight, casual wear, with sweaters and jackets for evenings and alpine heights, are the most appropriate clothing for this time of the year.

Winter Winters are cold in Korea and last from mid-November until March. In January and February, temperatures dip to between −12° and 2°C (10° and 35°F). Visitors should bring heavy woollen clothing (including a winter overcoat), and long underwear if excursions to national mountain parks are included.

While casual sportswear is appropriate for most occasions in Korea, you should also bring at least one dress-jacket or full-length dress. Koreans tend to dress up for formal banquets and other social occasions at night, especially in Seoul. It is also important to know that backless dresses, halter-tops, hot-pants, cut-off jeans and other exposing clothing are definitely not appropriate for public wear in Korea's conservative Confucian society.

Health

No vaccinations or inoculations are currently required for entry to Korea.

It is a good idea to avoid drinking water from the tap, except in major hotels where a special faucet for drinking water is provided. Medical care in Korea is modern and efficient; there are many good hospitals in Seoul. In addition, most international hotels retain a house doctor on the premises. Pharmacies in Korea are well stocked with modern medicines and are carefully monitored by government authorities.

Money

The unit of Korean currency is the *won*, which comes in coin denominations of W1, W10, W50, W100 and W500, and in banknotes of W500, W1,000, W5,000 and W10,000. Foreign banknotes and travellers cheques may be converted into *won* at foreign exchange banks and other authorized money changers and if you retain your receipts, you may change excess *won* back into foreign currency upon departure at the airport.

Internationally recognized credit cards such as Visa, American Express, Diners Club and MasterCard are accepted at major hotels, department stores, big tourist shops and some restaurants.

You may bring any amount of foreign currency into Korea, but amounts in excess of US$10,000 must be declared on arrival.

Banking hours in Korea are 9.30 am to 4.30 pm on weekdays and 9.30 am to 1.30 pm on Saturdays.

Tipping is not generally expected in Korea. A ten percent service charge is added to all hotel bills and most restaurant bills. Taxi drivers don't require tips, unless they perform a special service, such as carrying your bags, but they always appreciate small change. In addition, you should always leave a cash tip in *kisaeng* houses, drinking salons and similar establishments which provide hostess services. Unless specifically prohibited, bellhops generally receive W150 per bag.

Transportation

Domestic Air Service

Domestic air services are handled exclusively by Korean Airlines, which schedules over 100 flights per week between Seoul and Pusan (50 minutes), Cheju Island (55 minutes), Taegu (50 minutes) and other popular domestic destinations. For reservations and information, visit KAL's head office in Seoul at the KAL Building (118, 2-ka, Namdaemun Road, Chung-ku) or call KAL at 756−2000. To make KAL bookings elsewhere in Korea, call the following numbers: Pusan 44−0131; Taegu 423−4231; Sokcho 33−03311; Cheju 2−6111; Kwangju 232−0551 and Chinju 53−3906.

You are required to re-confirm all domestic reservations at least 24 hours prior to departure. Packages under 15 kilograms (33 pounds) are transported free of charge. Strict security measures are enforced on all domestic flights. For example, cameras, radios and even liquor (as a flammable liquid) cannot be carried in the passenger cabins, but must be placed in special containers in the cargo-hold and picked up at your destination.

Trains

Korean National Railroads maintains an extensive network of railways which connects far-flung points throughout the peninsula with Seoul and other major cities. Korea's first railroad service was inaugurated in September 1899, and prior to the Korean War you could actually travel from Pusan all the way to Paris by train. The railway network suffered serious damage during the Korean War, but since 1953, railroads in Korea have once again been expanded and modernized.

Korean National Railroads currently offers five types of railway service — *wanhaeng:* 'locals' which stop at every station along the way; *potong kuphaeng:* regular express trains with numerous stops, night service, and sleeping berths available; *tukkup:* limited express trains which sometimes have a dining car and offer advanced reservations for seats; *udung:* trains with air-conditioned (or heated) cars and *Saemaul:* super-express trains with air-conditioning (or heating) and dining cars.

Whenever possible, foreign travellers should opt for the fast *Saemaul* super-express, which now operates between Seoul and Taegu (four hours), Kyongju (4.5 hours), Pusan (4 hours 50 minutes) and Mokpo (5 hours 40 minutes), with several stops en route. Not only is *Saemaul* service the fastest and most comfortable in Korea, it also runs punctually.

Seats may be reserved and tickets purchased up to ten days in advance of scheduled departures, and it is a good idea to do this, especially during the summer, when many Koreans on vacation utilize railway transport. Reservations and advance ticket sales may be arranged at railway stations or through local travel and tourist agencies. Korean National Railroad's main office is located at 168, 2-ka, Bongraedong, Chung-ku in Seoul, tel. 392−7811. For information and reservations in Pusan call 463−5782, Kyongju 2−7788, Taejon 253−7451 and Yongju 2−1330.

Subways

Seoul's subway system opened in August 1974, and recently underwent major expansion to accommodate the expected massive crowds for the 1988 Olympics. Subways currently connect Seoul with four major destinations: Chongnyang-ni train station and Songbuk district to the north, Inchon to the west and Suwon to the south. Trains run every five minutes, and smoking is not permitted in the cars. The six subway stations within Seoul City, and the city sights to which they give access, are: Seoul Train Station, City Hall (Toksu Palace, Myong-dong district, major downtown hotels, department stores and government offices), Chonggak (Chogye Temple, Kyongbok Palace, KNTC Head Office, Sejong Cultural Centre), Chong-no, 3-ka (Pagoda Park, Chongmyo Royal Confucian Ancestral Shrine, Insadong), Chong-no, 5-ka, (Great East Gate Market, herbal medicine shops), and Tongdaemun (Great East Gate, Seoul Stadium).

Buses
Local City Buses Getting around Seoul by bus during heavy commuter rush hours can be a frustrating experience. At other times it is a convenient and inexpensive means of inner-city transportation. Fares are fixed regardless of distance: each token costs W120. Transfers are not given, and smoking is prohibited on board. Buses run frequently between 5 am and midnight.

Airport Shuttles A daily express shuttle-bus operates between Seoul's Kimpo Airport and the following downtown destinations: Sheraton Walker Hill Hotel, Seoul Garden Hotel, KAL City Terminal, Koreana Hotel, Seoul Plaza Hotel, Tokyu Hotel, Hyatt Hotel, Tower Hotel, Shilla Hotel and Hilton Hotel.

The airport shuttle departs from the Sheraton Walker Hill every 20 minutes, commencing at 6 am and terminating at 8.10 pm. It leaves every 10 minutes from the airport between 7.30 am and 9.30 pm. The one-way fare is W500.

Highway Express Buses Highway express buses connect all major cities in Korea, and ten express bus companies currently operate 1,768 buses on Korea's excellent highway system. There are three types of highway bus service: *kosok* is the fast super-express; *chikhaeng* is first class local service and *wanhaeng* is the regular local express with frequent stops along the way.

Although Korea's highway express buses are extremely fast and quite comfortable, some travellers avoid them due to accidents caused by speeding; nonetheless, there are rarely seats vacant.

Travellers are advised to reserve seats and purchase tickets for highway express buses in advance for holiday and weekend travel. All express bus services from Seoul to other cities originate at the Kangnam Kosok Express Bus Terminal, located across the Han River in Banpo-dong. Other major bus terminals in Seoul, which have regular bus service to less distant destinations are: Tongbu Bus

Terminal (tel. 792-3791), in Majang-dong (Chunchon, Mt Sorak,
Sokcho, Yangyang, Yongmun Temple, Kangnung, Yoju, Chungju,
Kwangju, Wonju and Andong); Nambu Bus Terminal (tel. 966-6762),
on the main road in south Yongsan (Kanghwa Island, Kosam, Taechon
Beach, Puyo, Kongju, Chonju, Mt Songni, Chonju and Taechon);
Shinchon Bus Terminal (tel. 34-0611), at the Shinchon Rotary
(Kanghwa Island); Miari Bus Terminal (tel. 980-7638) (Mt Soyo);
Chonho-dong Bus Terminal (tel. 48-2159), southeast of Seoul
(Southern Han Mountain Fortress — Namhansansong — and
Kwangju); Yok Chon Bus Terminal, across the street from the Seoul
Train Station behind the Greyhound Terminal (Suwon, Inchon, and
Pyongtaek); and Seoul Sobu Bus Terminal (tel. 388-5103), in
Pulgwang-dong (Haenju, Sansong, and Uichongbu).

Car Rentals and Taxis
Taxis are the most convenient mode of metropolitan transportation in
Seoul and other major Korean cities. Simply hail an empty cab on the
street, or call one from one of Seoul's 25 'call-taxi' companies. Regular
taxis currently charge W600 for the first two kilometres (1.2 miles),
and W50 for each additional 400 metres (0.25 mile). During rush
hours, these taxis often pick up three or four unrelated riders,
dropping each one off at his destination and charging him only for his
portion of the ride. Call cabs cost W1,000 for the first two kilometres
(1.2 miles) and W100 for each additional 400 metres (0.25 mile). Call
cabs may be readily summoned for you by the doorman or service desk
of any hotel, or you may call directly for one at 414-0150/9.
      By far the best way to see Korea is by private car, either with a
chauffeur-driven or self-driven vehicle. Four excellent expressways
criss-cross the Korean peninsula: Kyongbu (Seoul-Pusan); Honam
(Taechon-Kwangju); Yongdong (Suwon-Kangnung) and Namhae
(Kwangju-Sunchon-Masan-Pusan). These expressways and their
ancillary county roads cut through Korea's most scenic mountains,
valley and farmland and are a pleasure to drive.
      The high cost of private cars and gasoline in Korea may inflate the
traveller's budget, but it has the distinct advantage of keeping highway
traffic to an absolute minimum. Driving along Korea's scenic
highways, the only traffic one generally encounters are commercial
trucks and convoys of speeding highway buses. So if you can afford it,
see Korea by car.
      Korea Rent-a-Car, in affiliation with America's Hertz Rent-a-Car,
is the major car rental agency in Seoul, with over 200 cars available.
Hertz-Korean's main office is in Hannamdong (tel. 585-0801/4), with
branch offices at Kimpo Airport's Information Counter, the lobbies of

the Chosun and Lotte Hotels, and Sodae-mun (next to the Red Cross Hospital). Drivers must be at least 21 years old and must present their passports as well as valid international or foreign driving licenses. Elsewhere in Korea, call the following numbers: Pusan: Yongnam Rent-a-Car 44-5000; Kyongju: Samjin Rent-a-Car 42-3311; Taegu: Yong-il Rent-a-Car 952-0001; and Cheju: Cheju Rent-a-Car 42-3301. Self-drive rentals in Korea permit unlimited mileage, and include insurance. Current fees are in the range of W29,000−36,000. Weekly rates are less expensive. Gas costs about US$6.00 per gallon — over four times the cost in America.

Fees for chauffeur-driven vehicles include the driver, gasoline, insurance and tax, but not highway tolls and parking fees. Basic rental fees range from W24,600−33,000 for three hours to W49,000−66,000 for ten hours. Excess charges come to W140 per kilometre (0.6 mile) or W2,600 per hour.

Those who wish to make side-trips outside Seoul by private cars may ask a hotel clerk to negotiate a flat rate for a whole day with a local taxi driver.

Ferries
Numerous ferries and private fishing boats provide regular service between Korea's coastal towns and off-shore islands.

The most scenic domestic ferryboat services in Korea are briefly described below:

Hallyo Waterway Two hydrofoil ferries run between Pusan and various points in the scenic Hallyo Waterway. The *Angel Ho* runs from Pusan to Chungmu six times a day, with a stop at Songpo. It runs from Chungmu over to Yosu three times a day, with stops at Samchonpo and Namhae. Pusan to Chungmu takes 1.5 hours, and Chungmu to Yosu takes one hour 40 minutes.

The *Venus Ho* runs once a day at 1 pm from Pusan to Yosu, with stops at Songpo, Chungmu, Samchonpo and Namhae. It returns daily along the same route, departing Yosu at 7.50 am. The one-way trip takes four hours 10 minutes.

For tickets and information in Seoul, call 734-5636. In Pusan, call 44-3851. Local travel and tour agencies can make ferryboat reservations on your behalf.

Pusan/Cheju Island The *Tongyang Kosok Ho* express car-ferry operates regular non-stop service between Pusan and Cheju Island in both directions. It departs Pusan every Monday, Wednesday and Friday at 7.30 pm, and leaves Cheju for the return trip on Tuesday, Thursday and Saturday at 7 pm. The one-way trip takes 11 hours.

For reservations and information in Seoul, call 730-7788, in Pusan 463-0605 and in Cheju 22-0291, or ask a local travel agent to make arrangements.

Pohang/Ullung Island During the peak summer season, the *Hanil Ho* express ferry operates a daily service between Pohang and Ullung Island, departing Pohang at 3.30 pm and returning from Ullung at 6.30 am. During the rest of the year, the *Hanil Ho* departs from Pohang and Ullung on alternate days at 10 am. The 195-kilometre (121-mile) journey takes six hours, and first-class accommodation includes such comforts as soft reclining seats, air-conditioning and television. Advanced reservations and tickets may be arranged by telephoning the Hanil Ho office in Seoul at 598-2101.

Wando/Cheju From Wando, one may travel by sea to Cheju Island by taking the *Hanil 2 Ho* ferry, which departs Wando for Cheju daily at 4 pm. The crossing takes two hours. Call 598-2101 in Seoul, 2238 in Wando and 22-4170 in Cheju.

Mokpo/Cheju One may also boat directly between Mokpo and Cheju Island by taking the *Tongyang* ferry, which makes a daily run from Mokpo at 4 pm, except Sundays. The journey takes six hours. Reservations and tickets for this boat may be arranged by calling the ferry office in Mokpo at 2-9391, in Cheju at 22-0291 or in Seoul at 730-7788.

Communication

Korea is a modern country with up-to-date postal and telecommunication facilities.

Mail

Seoul's central post office is located on Chungmu Road, a block east of Shinsegye Department Store, just across from the Taiwanese Embassy. There are branch offices conveniently located near the intersection of Taepyong and Chong Streets, and on Yulkok Street near the Anguk Immigration Office. Stamps are also available in most hotels and at many licensed shops around town.

Regular stamped letters or postcards may be dropped in any mail-box or posted at any post office, but all overseas parcels must be mailed and picked up at the International Post Office across from Yonsei University in Yonhi-dong. All incoming and outgoing mail in Korea is subject to government inspection. Delivery time to and from Europe and America is 9–14 days, while local mail takes two to three days for delivery. Post office hours are 9 am until 5 pm Monday through Friday, and 9 am until 1 pm on Saturday.

Telephone
Local Calls Local calls may be dialled from the red and green
telephones located in hotels, public buildings and phone-booths. Calls
within the city require two W10 coins, and all local calls are
automatically terminated after three minutes. For longer
conversations, hang up, deposit two more coins, and dial again.

Long-Distance Calls Within Korea One may dial directly to any
point within Korea by using the large yellow pay-phones located in
hotels, post offices, and elsewhere. These phones have slots for both
W10 and W100 coins, and you should have sufficient change in hand
before dialling. When you hear bleeps over the line, put more coins
into the phone, otherwise you will get cut off. You may talk as long as
you wish, as long as you continue putting coins in the slot. Extra coins
are automatically returned when you hang up.

Overseas Calls One may place international calls through the
operator at major hotels, or at the International Telecommunications
Exchange, located on Sejong Road near the Sejong Cultural Centre.
To place international calls from private phones in Seoul, dial 1035 or
1037 to get the overseas operator. International Subscriber Dialling
(ISD) connects Korea with 75 countries. The ISD access code is
reached by dialing 001. Korea's ISD country code is 82 and the Seoul
area code is 02.

Telegrams
One may send international telegrams from the International
Telecommunications Building on Sejong Road, or by dialling 115 on
the phone and dictating the message in English.

Korea offers three types of telegram service: 'Urgent' takes six
hours; 'Ordinary' takes 12 hours; and 'Letter Telegram' (LT) requires
24 hours to reach its destination.

The International Telecommunications Building is open from 9 am
until 5 pm Monday through Friday, and 9 am until 1 pm on Saturday.

Radio and Television
Four major Korean radio stations broadcast programmes throughout
the country, with various affiliates in the more heavily populated areas.
In addition, American Forces Korea Network (AFKN) operates eight
transmitters which broadcast programmes and popular music 24 hours
a day throughout the country (except Cheju Island). AFKN
programmes are broadcast entirely in English, with international news
reports on the hour.

There are two Korean television broadcasting networks, with
affiliates throughout the country. They are Korea Broadcasting Service
(KBS-TV) and Munhwa Broadcasting Company (MBC-TV).

Newspapers

Six nationally distributed newspapers are currently published in Korea, including one in Chinese and two in English. They appear daily, except for Mondays and major national holidays. The two English-language newspapers are *The Korea Herald* and *The Korea Times*. They are available in hotels, bookstores and newsstands throughout the country.

Time Zone

Korea lies within the same time zone as Japan. When it is noon in Korea it is 7 pm the day before in San Francisco, 10 pm the day before in New York, 3 am the same day in Paris and 10 am the same day in Bangkok.

The Land and the People

The Korean peninsula juts out like a spur from the Asian mainland, just below Manchuria and eastern Siberia. Lying between 43 and 34 degrees north, Korea is approximately the size of Great Britain or New York State and stretches 1,000 kilometres (620 miles) north to south, and 216 kilometres (134 miles) east to west at its narrowest point. The communist North occupies about 122,000 square kilometres (48,000 square miles) of Korea, while the South is slightly smaller at 99,000 square kilometres (38,000 miles). To the west lie the Yellow Sea and China, to the east lie the East Sea and Japan. Scattered off the rugged coastline of Korea are over 3,000 islands.

Korea is a land of mountains. Wherever you set your gaze, you can see ridge upon ridge of rugged, low-rising mountains rolling away into the horizon. Because it is so hilly, Korea has been described as 'a country which stands on end'. Only 20 percent of the country consists of arable farmland.

Korea is ribboned with short, swift-flowing rivers originating in her many mountains. These twisting, often treacherous rivers provide the land with ample water but little viable inland navigation. The west coast, washed by the shifting waters of the Yellow Sea, is riddled with shallow, narrow inlets with tidal changes ranging from five to eight metres (17 to 26 feet). The east coast, ribbed by the magnificent Diamond Mountains, falls abruptly to the East Sea, where it forms fine swimming beaches and fertile fishing coves.

Nearly barren only 30 years ago, the entire country is currently under intensive reforestation, especially in the mountain parks and popular resort areas. Native trees include the beloved pine and juniper, bamboo and willow, rich red maples and flowering fruit trees such as apricot, peach, plum and cherry. New growth is complemented everywhere by beautifully landscaped gardens alive with seasonal blossoms such as azalea, forsythia, cosmos and Rose of Sharon, the national flower. Now into its third decade, this reforestation programme has made the entire country a colourful tapestry of changing hues, especially during spring and autumn.

Korea is home to many exotic breeds of birds and host to a variety of migrating species seldom seen elsewhere. Formerly close to extinction, many of these species have gained a new lease of life in Korea due to strenuous conservation efforts. Ironically, the bleak and barren DMZ which separates North from South Korea has in recent years become a haven for the magnificent Manchurian Crane, once presumed to be teetering on the brink of extinction. This big beautiful bird, whose snow-white plumage is adorned with a red feather cap and

black-trimmed wings, has been revered for millennia in China, Korea, and Japan as the supreme symbol of longevity. Perhaps its miraculous reappearance along the world's most volatile border will serve both sides as an auspicious omen of peace.

The population of Korea is currently at about 40 million, with an annual growth rate of 1.5 percent. Evidence suggests that the Korean peninsula was first settled by migrant tribes from northern and central Asia about 30,000 years ago. Over the ages, Koreans developed a unique, homogeneous culture of their own, including their own language, cuisine, and manner of dress. Physically, Korean men are somewhat taller, deeper chested and more robust than their Chinese and Japanese neighbours, while Korean women are small and lissome like other Asian women. The most distinctive physical traits of most Koreans, men and women alike, are strong hands and thick wrists.

The Korean language and way of life grew from the ancient Altaic culture which once thrived from the Russian Urals all the way across central Asia to Siberia, long before the time of Confucius, Buddha or Christ. Korea was the easternmost outpost of Altaic culture, which put a permanent stamp on Korean life. Even today, the Korean language resembles Finnish and Turkish more than it does Chinese or Japanese. This Altaic heritage has been the underlying cohesive force binding Koreans together through three millennia of turbulent history and foreign intrusion.

However, in outward appearance and behaviour, Koreans today reflect the Chinese, Japanese and Western influences which have moulded their recent history. Unlike the Chinese, however, Koreans maintain strict public decorum and reverent formality among themselves. Yet, unlike the rigid, introverted and impenetrable Japanese, Koreans are very warm, emotional and quick to laugh. Though always poised and polite in public, they can become most passionate in private. In the Korean culture, poise and passion balance like *yin* and *yang*, and each has its own place and time.

National pride is deeply ingrained in the Korean character. This trait, rather than being the jingoistic style of patriotism so often displayed in the world, is the deeply felt love of an ancient people for their land and heritage, a love that transcends contemporary government and politics and embraces the very spirit of Korea. This national pride is most movingly manifested by the reverent appreciation which Koreans often express for the natural beauties of their land, for the great feats of their historical heroes and for the subtle aesthetics of their traditional culture.

By far the best way to understand the Korean character is to try to feel rather than fathom it.

A Turbulent History

Like all ancient cultures, Korea has its own legend of creation. Long ago, Hwanung, son of the divine creator, descended from Heaven to Earth and proclaimed himself king of 'everything under Heaven'. As he surveyed his earthly domain, he heard the fervent prayers of a bear who wished to become human. So Hwanung gave the bear 20 pieces of garlic and some mugwort and told it to retire to a cave for 100 days. The bear emerged as the first human woman.

This woman then prayed for a son, soon became pregnant by divine grace, and gave birth to Tan'gun, the first human king and the founder of Korea. Tan'gun is said to have founded Korea in 2333 BC and ruled until 1027 BC.

In 1027, King Kija arrived and established a new dynasty in Chosun. The legend says that Kija was a direct descendant of China's ancient Shang Dynasty, which fell in dissolution to the house of Zhou that very same year.

Korea's foundation legend is interesting for two reasons: first, the role of garlic and mugwort in transforming the bear into a woman reflects the vital role that garlic and herbal medicine have played in Korean culture since prehistoric times. Second, the date 1027 BC, which marked the establishment of new dynasties in both China and Korea, establishes a very early connection between historical events in these two neighbouring countries. Such parallels have continued down to the present day.

The Chinese Connection

After the establishment of the Han Dynasty in China in 206 BC, Korea's historical record grows clearer. During its heyday, Han China ruled the entire northern portion of the Korean peninsula, but when the Han Dynasty disintegrated around AD 200, an alliance of Korean tribes known as Koguryo rose to power and wrested control of northern Korea and southeastern Manchuria from the Chinese. Koguryo remained ethnically and culturally Korean, but in its rise to power, it wisely adopted advanced Chinese military and administrative systems.

Meanwhile, further south on the Korean peninsula, two powerful tribes emerged: the Paekche carved a kingdom out of the south-western corner, and the Silla established a kingdom which held dominion over the entire southeastern portion of the peninsula. Like the three kingdoms which supplanted the Han Dynasty in China, these three Korean kingdoms engaged in constant internecine warfare, devious political intrigues and rapidly shifting alliances. Here the second great parallel to Chinese history emerges, for in both Korea and China this period is known as 'the Three Kingdoms Period', and in both countries it was a time of political turbulence and intellectual ferment.

In AD 618, in China, the house of Tang defeated all other rivals for the dragon-throne and reunited the Chinese empire for the first time since the fall of Han. One of the Tang Dynasty's first objectives was to establish effective control over the Korean peninsula. In 645 and again in 647, Tang armies attacked the Koguryo kingdom but failed to conquer it. So, adopting the age-old Chinese political strategy of 'using barbarians to subdue barbarians', the Tang court allied itself with the southern Silla kingdom, and together Tang and Silla defeated first Paekche in 660, then Koguryo in 667. Not satisfied, Tang China next tried to vanquish its Silla ally as well. ·

But Silla declined to play the role of China's political pawn and rebelled against Tang authority, giving aid and encouragement to insurgents in Paekche and Koguryo as well. The three heroic unifiers of Korea — King Muyol, his successor King Minmu and their military commander General Kim — fought against overwhelming odds to drive the Chinese back across the Taedon River and unify the entire Korean peninsula under the banner of Silla. Silla succeeded in establishing dominion over Paekche and Koguryo, and the Chinese, much to their chagrin, were driven out of Korea. An agreement was then reached which saved China's face on the one hand and ensured Silla's future security and independence on the other. Silla would remain an independent Korean kingdom, but it would also become an official tributary state of China.

Silla and Koryo

Historians generally regard Silla's unification of the Korean peninsula in the seventh century as the beginning of Korea's history as a united nation. Though this unity sometimes proved chimerical in subsequent centuries, it persisted more or less intact until the country was politically partitioned between North and South in 1945.

During the Silla Dynasty, Korea began to exert profound influence on Japan, which till then had remained tribal and uncivilized. Some historians attribute the rise of Yamato, Japan's first unified state, to the arrival of aristocratic horse-riding invaders from Korea. Korean scholars became the personal tutors of Japan's first royal house; they included the famous Prince Shotoku, to whom so much early Japanese culture is attributed. Koreans held important administrative posts in the emerging Japanese nation, and in Japan's official family registry of AD 815, fully one-third of the noble families listed are of Korean descent. There are numerous royal burial mounds in Japan which to this day lie unexcavated, despite the deep curiosity of archaeologists and historians the world over, who believe that these mounds contain valuable artefacts which verify Japan's deep cultural debt to Korea. But because Japanese intellectuals are loathe to recognize this influence, the tombs remain untouched.

As the Tang Dynasty in China began to crumble during the ninth century, so did Silla. Various branches of the royal clan plotted for power, peasant revolts broke out, and bandits ran rampant throughout the country. Then, just about the time that the house of Song reunified China, the house of Koryo re-established unity in Korea and founded a dynasty in AD 935 that was to last 450 years.

The Koryo Dynasty, from which the word 'Korea' is derived, was founded by Wang Kon, who was the son of a merchant. Wang Kon invoked the Chinese concept of the Mandate of Heaven, whereby a new ruler justified his ascendancy to the throne on moral rather than hereditary grounds. This was a first in Korean history. Wang Kon also adopted other Chinese government institutions, such as a centralized bureaucracy and standard civil service examinations. But both the exams and the jobs remained open only to the families of Korea's ruling elite.

Koryo kings generously patronized Buddhism, and under their royal auspices it became a powerful force in Korean affairs. Monks appeared frequently in court and took active roles in politics. Buddhist temples, pagodas and statuary sprouted up throughout the Korean peninsula. During the early years of the Koryo era, celadon porcelain reached its zenith of craftsmanship, and by the 14th century Korea had begun to print books with moveable type, 200 years before the method was invented in Europe.

In 1231, Ghenghis Khan's Mongol Alliance attacked Korea in full force but met with unexpectedly stiff resistance. Meanwhile, the Koryo court retreated into exile on Kanghwa Island, and there the king ordered the engraving of the Tripitaka Koreana on 80,000 wooden tablets, based on the original and complete Chinese translation of the Buddhist scriptures. On completion, this massive tome was burned as an offering to the gods in hopes of securing their aid against the Mongols. Later, another complete set of 80,000 wood blocks was inscribed, and this collection still remains in storage at the Haein Temple near Taegu.

By 1279 Koryo and the Mongol Khans managed to reach a political accommodation which preserved at least a semblance of independence

for Korea, but the price exacted was high. Koryo's crown princes were required to reside in the new Chinese capital at Beijing, marry Mongol princesses, and remain hostage there until reigning Koryo kings died. The Mongols also demanded heavy annual tribute from Korea in gold, silver, ginseng and women. Thus, the Mongols established effective control over the Koryo kingdom, and Mongol queens often wielded more power than Koryo kings.

The Yi Dynasty

The Ming Dynasty was established in China in 1368, when Chinese rebels under the leadership of the peasant general Chu Yuan-chang drove the Mongols back north across the Great Wall. Twenty years later, a Ming army was dispatched to conquer Korea, and the Koryo court responded by sending a fiery young commander named Yi Song-gye to repel the invaders.

Yi, knowing that his army stood no chance of success against superior Ming forces, turned back instead and deposed the King of Koryo. In 1392, Yi invoked the Mandate of Heaven and established the Yi Dynasty, Korea's last and longest dynasty, which ended only when Japan annexed Korea in 1910. Yi immediately re-established traditional tributary relations with Ming China, adopted Neo-Confucianism as the new state creed, and named his kingdom *Chosun*, the 'Land of Morning Calm', China's ancient name for Korea. He also moved the kingdom's capital to Hanyang; the city today is known as Seoul.

King Sejong, the fourth Yi ruler, who reigned from 1418 to 1450, is generally regarded as Korea's greatest king. During his reign Korean culture flourished as never before, and men of merit were placed in the highest bureaucratic offices. It was King Sejong who supervised the development of *hangul*, the unique Korean alphabet which freed Korean writing and education from its cumbersome dependence on complex Chinese ideograms.

Korea's hard-earned domestic calm was soon shattered by outside events. This time the intrusion came from Japan, when the powerful warlord Hideyoshi launched his mad campaign to conquer China in 1592. At first he invited Korea to join him in the campaign, but when the Yi court declined to attack its friendly neighbour, Hideyoshi sent an army of 150,000 men to punish Korea. Japanese forces swept across the peninsula and subdued Korea in less than a month.

But the Japanese were not at all prepared for Admiral Yi Sun-sin and his armada of Turtle Ships. Admiral Yi was a skilled naval tactician, a loyal Korean patriot and an orthodox Confucian gentleman. The Turtle Ships he developed — compact, highly manoeuverable fighting ships propelled by oar and heavily armed with cannon — were the world's first armour-plated warships. Their decks and gunwales were covered with spike-studded sheets of heavy iron, making them virtually invulnerable to enemy projectiles and boardings. Yi and his handful of Turtle Ships panicked the Japanese fleet, and sank over 250 enemy ships in eight battles, forcing the Japanese to withdraw from Korea before even setting foot in China.

Hideyoshi was infuriated by Korean resistance and launched another attack in 1598. In the meantime, Admiral Yi had fallen victim to Korean court intrigues and was dismissed as naval commander. His successor sallied forth to meet the second Japanese onslaught and promptly lost all but a dozen of Korea's naval ships. Yi was quickly recalled to duty and with only a dozen ships under his command, he once again routed the numerically superior Japanese fleet, sinking or capturing most of their ships and setting the rest to flight. In November 1598, as Admiral Yi surveyed the final battle of the war from the bow of his flagship, a stray bullet struck his chest and killed him. His last command to his lieutenants was to conceal his death from his men until victory was assured. To this day, Admiral Yi remains Korea's greatest military hero, and numerous statues of him clad in battle attire are to be seen throughout the land.

Hideyoshi's death in 1598 ended Japan's campaign to conquer China and Korea, but once again Korea's calm was short-lived.

In 1644, the Manchus decisively defeated the Ming, occupied Beijing, and established China's last dynasty, the Qing. Korea became a tributary state of the Qing Dynasty and remained so until Japan wrested control of Korea from China at the turn of the century, and annexed the peninsula in 1910. Interestingly, both China's and Korea's last dynasties fell within a year of one another.

The Hermit Kingdom

After the consecutive traumas of Japanese and Manchu invasions, the Yi court enforced a strict 'closed door' policy towards all foreigners except the Chinese. Korea became the 'Hermit Kingdom', insular and aloof. But as the 19th century approached and the country's protector, the Qing Dynasty, declined, there was little Korea could do to forestall its fate.

Catholic misssionaries arrived through Beijing. The Yi court considered their teachings a subversive threat to Confucian order and in 1866 nine French Catholic priests were publicly executed and 8,000 of their Korean converts were massacred in the ensuing pogroms.

Throughout the 19th century, Korea continued to rebuff European and American efforts to establish diplomatic and commercial ties. Japan took offence at the exclusion policy and in 1875 deliberately created an incident between Japanese naval ships and Korean shore defences. Taking its cue from Western 'gunboat diplomacy', Japan used the ensuing peace negotiations to force Korea into permitting Japanese diplomatic and trade missions to be established on Korean soil.

The Japanese Conquest

Japanese influence on the Korean peninsula grew rapidly during the late 19th century, much to the dismay of the Korean government, which was nominally still a tributary of China. China reacted by sending reinforcements into Korea to reassert Chinese authority. During the early 1880s Chinese and Japanese forces clashed several times on Korean soil.

The cumulative effects of aggressive foreign pressures — Japanese, Chinese, as well as Western — led directly to the Tonghak Uprising of 1894, which in turn sparked the Sino-Japanese War. The Tonghak (Eastern Learning) Movement was a grass-roots religious and social campaign which proposed a blend of traditional Eastern learning to combat and expel foreign influence and save Korea from ruin. A small peasant uprising in Cholla Province quickly led to major rebel victories over government forces. The government promptly petitioned China for help. When China sent an army across the Yalu to help suppress the revolt, Japan responded instantly by sending its own army into Korea, uninvited.

Chinese and Japanese forces again tangled on Korean soil, sparking the Sino-Japanese War. Japan dealt the decadent court of China a swift and humiliating defeat, forcing China to accept the terms of the notorious Treaty of Shimonoseki, which formally ended hostilities on 17 April 1895. This treaty guaranteed Korea's 'independence' from China and gave Japan a stranglehold over Korean affairs, a role which led to outright annexation 15 years later. Japan also demanded and received complete control of the Ryukyu Islands (Okinawa) and Taiwan as part of the deal, and they formally annexed these islands the same year.

In the Russian-Japanese War of 1904, the Russians too were trounced by Japan's emerging military strength and in the wake of that victory Japan immediately occupied all of Korea. The Treaty of Portsmouth, which ended hostilities on 5 September 1905, gave Japan's control over Korea international recognition.

Korean patriots offered stiff resistance to Japanese occupation and formed guerilla bands to harass the intruders. In 1909, the Japanese resident-general Ito Hirobumi was assassinated by a Korean patriot while visiting Harbin, Manchuria. In retaliation, Japan dictated a new treaty on 22 August 1910, in which Korea was formally annexed and Korean statehood completely abolished.

Japan launched a cruel campaign to eradicate Korean culture and replace it with Japanese models. Korea's beloved ancient palaces and temples were razed and bulldozed, and famous masters of native Korean arts were interned or killed to prevent them from spreading traditional Korean culture to a new generation. Korean history was summarily dropped from school curricula, and all courses were subsequently taught in Japanese. Koreans were forced to adopt Japanese names, Japanese language and Japanese manners. Thousands of Korean men were pressed into Japan's armed forces or shipped *en masse* to Japan as virtual slave-labourers, while Korean women were rounded up by the hundreds to serve as playthings for Japan's occupation troops.

The Korean War

In August 1945, Japan surrendered to the Allies, ending World War II, and withdrew its forces from the Korean peninsula. Koreans celebrated in the belief that their long-lost independence was finally restored, but it soon became clear that Russia and America had very different ideas regarding the future of Korea. In order to forestall immediate confrontations between the occupying forces of the United States and the Soviet Union, the 38th Parallel was selected as a 'temporary' line of demarcation between the two hostile sides. The Russians went straight to work establishing a full-fledged communist regime in the North, with Kim Il-sung as their surrogate, while the Americans withdrew from the South, leaving it in political disarray.

In September 1947 the United Nations called for the establishment of a united and independent Korean state and suggested that national elections be held to choose a suitable government. The Soviet Union, however, refused to permit the UN to supervise elections in the North; they were held only in the South. On 15 August 1948 the Republic of Korea was declared in the South, with Syngman Rhee as its first president and Seoul as its capital. The Soviet-controlled North reacted by declaring the establishment of the Democratic Republic of Korea on 9 September 1948, with Kim Il-sung as head of state and Pyongyang as the capital. For the first time since the Silla Dynasty had united the Three Kingdoms during the seventh century, Korea was divided into two hostile political entities.

A tiger depicted in traditional style. Tigers were rampant in Korea until the early 20th century.

37

By the end of 1948, both Russian and American troops had been withdrawn from the two Koreas. However, the Russians continued to funnel arms and advisers into the North, building up a formidable North Korean army, while the United States did very little to improve South Korean military power. In January 1950, the American Secretary of State made a public statement in which he declared that the Korean situation lay outside America's vital interests and beyond the line of American defences. This new stance, as well as the growing military disparity between the two Koreas, led the North to believe that it could conquer the South by force of arms.

On 25 June 1950, North Korean troops stormed across the 38th Parallel in a massive, full-scale invasion of the South. Due to the absence of the Soviet delegate to the United Nations, the United States managed to secure a UN resolution branding the North Koreans as aggressors and pledging UN support in defence of the South. Although 16 nations ultimately sent troops to fight in the Korean War, the overwhelming majority of soldiers was American.

At first the North Korean invaders routed South Korean defences, nearly driving them off the peninsula. Then the American commander, General Douglas MacArthur, conceived and successfully executed a daring amphibious landing at Inchon, cutting off the over-extended North Korean forces and effectively turning the tide of war against them. Despite strong warnings from China not to cross the demarcation line, MacArthur pursued the enemy across the 38th Parallel deep into North Korea.

As US forces rapidly approached the Manchurian border, Chinese troops suddenly poured across the Yalu River in vast human waves, sending UN troops staggering back across the 38th Parallel, and recapturing Seoul. Bloody battles raged back and forth across the peninsula, with heavy casualties on both sides and massive destruction to the land.

Finally, on 27 July 1953, an armistice ended the fighting and formally divided Korea at the 38th Parallel, with a five-kilometre (three-mile) wide demilitarized zone (DMZ) in between. This belt of 'no man's land' is currently supervised by a joint North/South Military Armistice Commission, which has been meeting regularly since 1953 at Panmunjom to discuss alleged truce violations. To date, they are the longest ongoing truce talks in history.

An Uneasy Truce

At the end of the war, Seoul and most of the countryside lay in ruins, industry had ground to a halt and corruption was rampant. The government of President Syngam Rhee, staffed entirely by personal protégés, proved inept and became increasingly unpopular. In 1960, Rhee resigned from office and retired to Hawaii after massive demonstrations followed the obviously rigged elections which had returned him to power.

The new government was refreshingly liberal, but it was hopelessly weak and ineffective in dealing with Korea's pressing problems. It was toppled by a military coup on 16 May 1961, and before long Major-General Park Chung-hee emerged from behind the scenes as South Korea's new national leader. He called for elections in 1963, retired from the military and ran successfully for president.

Park won second and third terms in office in 1967 and 1971. To guarantee his strong hold over Korean affairs, he declared martial law on 17 October 1962, and took all effective political power into his own hands and ruled the country by decree. During Park's long, ambitious career at Korea's helm, the country began to perform economic miracles and — albeit through the suppression of dissent — there was social stability.

Park was assassinated in 1979. The next year, General Chun Tu-hwan was inaugurated as president. His policies were similar to those of Park, and Korea increasingly prospered whilst its society continued to be run with strict discipline.

The first half of 1987 saw large-scale anti-government protests, which prompted Roh Tae-woo, Chun's hand-picked successor, to announce that democratic reforms would be introduced. An amnesty proposed by Roh restored civil rights to some of the government's leading opponents and allowed the media to increase its coverage of opposition views. Many Koreans hope their country will be able to perform political miracles to match its economic success.

The transition to democracy will not be easy, however, for South Korea is in a state of continual preparedness for a resumption of the war with the North. The truce is fragile, and hundreds of violations have been recorded over the years.

It is this uneasy truce between North and South that constitutes the greatest hindrance to Korea's future and the greatest threat to peace in Northeast Asia. Like the leaders of the prosperous Silla Kingdom which first united Korea 1,400 years ago, leaders in Seoul today would like to see the entire Korean peninsula united in freedom, independence and economic prosperity, and until such reunification takes place, Korea's history is likely to remain turbulent.

Korean Arts and Culture

The traditional arts and culture of Korea offer penetrating insights into Korean character and clearly reflect the various strains which have influenced her history. The symbolism of shamanism and Taoism, the religious themes of Buddhism and the lofty ideals of Confucianism all found artistic expression in the skilled hands of Korean craftsmen.

Arts and Crafts

The manner in which a people design their private dwellings and public buildings is perhaps the most accurate reflection of their aesthetic tastes. Like Korean food and Korean costume, Korean architecture reflects the originality of Korean style. The hallmark of the traditional Korean home is the ubiquitous *ondol* (warm-floor) heating system, which has been in continuous use since the Stone Age. Underground flues circulate hot air from a central source, such as the kitchen stove or an underground fireplace, to a network of pipes beneath the floors. Once a room is warm, the temperature can be maintained all day and night with minimum expenditure of fuel. So comfortable are *ondol* floors with cushions that Koreans seldom make use of chairs.

The spark of inspiration for Korean temple and palace architecture came from China about 2,000 years ago, but Koreans gave the roofs a subtly different look. Chinese roofs emphasize a vertical sweep up towards heaven, and are generally elevated high off the ground. Korean architects gave their rooflines longer, more graceful curves that sweep low towards the earth, then flare slightly towards the sky at the four corners.

Paper production is one of Korea's most renowned crafts. First introduced from China about 1,000 years ago, papercraft was perfected by Koreans, and even today handmade Korean writing paper is highly prized by Chinese and Japanese calligraphers for its durability and special absorbent qualities. Paper for windows, screens, *ondol* floors, calligraphy and painting is still made by hand with traditional methods in the city of Chonju, where one may witness the entire process at Oh Dong-Ho's Paper Factory. Recently, what is billed as 'the world's oldest piece of paper' was discovered in Korea; it is a Buddhist manuscript dating from AD 754.

Over the centuries, Korean kilns have produced some of the world's finest porcelain, especially celadon. 'Celadon' refers to an iron-bearing glaze used by Koryo craftsmen to produce the characteristic blue-green colours associated with the best Korean porcelain. It reached its peak of perfection during the Koryo Dynasty (935–1392). Far more earthy and less contrived than Chinese designs, Koryo celadon is prized by collectors around the world for its natural lines and warm human touch. Simple designs were boldly executed with a few masterful strokes, a technique which the Japanese greatly admired and tried to emulate in their own ceramics. Korean craftsmen are also renowned for the long, elegant curves they create in ceramic ware — the spouts and handles on wine vessels, and tall, slim vases. During the Japanese invasion of Korea between 1592 and 1598, not only were entire collections of Korean porcelain shipped off to Japan, but whole villages of ceramic craftsmen were uprooted and taken to Japan, to lay the foundations for the Japanese ceramic industry.

Ancient Koreans also excelled at bronze-casting and metallurgy. Masters at casting bronze temple bells, they created the most sonorous and beautifully decorated bells in Asia. The oldest bronze bell in Korea was cast in AD 725 and now hangs at the Sangwon Temple in Mt Odae National Park. The most famous Korean bell is the melodious Emille Bell, which was cast in AD 771 and now hangs in a pavilion outside the Kyongju National Museum. The pipe-hole at the top is a unique feature of Korean bells and contributes to their remarkable clarity and resonance. It is said that on a calm day the Emille Bell can be clearly heard 68 kilometres (42 miles) away.

Korea's royal crowns represent the finest achievement of ancient Korean jewellers. The solid gold crowns of Silla's shaman kings dazzled the world when they were displayed recently as part of '5,000 Years of Korean Culture', a touring exhibit of Korean art and artefacts. The three-tiered pine trees, stylized reindeer horns, curved wings poised for flight and jade tiger-claw pendants on Korean crowns all reflect ancient shaman symbols from Korea's rich past. The only crown with similar characteristics discovered elsewhere in the world was unearthed in the Soviet Union and dates from the first century AD — a discovery which verifies Korea's intimate connections with the ancient Altaic culture that once flourished from northern Europe across Russia and Siberia to East Asia.

In the fields of painting and calligraphy, Korean artists were inspired by Chinese models but drew their themes from indigenous Korean culture. Koryo painting, for example, reflects a strong stylistic influence from Song China, but its thematic content is drawn from Korean Buddhism. Koryo painters excelled in depicting the transparency of drapery and robes in religious paintings, using light, subtle strokes in their work.

When the Yi Dynasty overthrew the Koryo and repressed Buddhism, religious painting was replaced by Confucian concepts of art. Elegant calligraphy and highly stylized landscape painting became popular. Auspicious Chinese ideograms such as those for 'long life',

'happiness', 'peace', 'prosperity' and 'health' appeared in stylized form on screens, scrolls, chests, porcelain and other items.
Certain themes and motifs crop up again and again in traditional Korean arts and crafts. The cosmic symbols of shamanism, for example, have appeared in Korean artwork ever since early times, and they continue to pervade Korean arts and crafts. In addition, many symbols from Chinese Taoism, first adopted in Korea before the

Shaman Roots

Shamanism is the deepest root of traditional Korean culture. Inherited from the ancient Altaic civilization which once flourished from Russia across northern Asia all the way to Korea, shamanism predates written history in Korea.

Shamanism is a form of animism, a common feature of all primitive and preliterate societies. Animists believe that spirits animate everything in nature, from water, rocks, and clouds to plants, animals and people. The function of shamans (mediums, medicine men, witch doctors) is to communicate with these spirits while in a deep trance and supplicate them for favourable action among the living.

While shamanism has faded from the scene in most societies, it remains very much alive in Korea, where it has survived as a result of the strict subordination of women under Confucianism. Shamanism, which sprang from a matriarchal society, provides an emotional and spiritual outlet for Korean women, especially during times of stress and frustration, which occur frequently in Korea's ultra-conservative Confucian society. Despite the country's formal acceptance of Buddhism, Confucianism and Christianity, shamanism continues to flourish in Korean society due to patronage of women from all walks of life. Traditional shamanist symbols pervade every aspect of Korean art, and Korean culture cannot be fully appreciated without a basic understanding of its deep shaman roots.

Ancient Altaic culture, for example, regarded the sun as a golden reindeer which rose daily in the east for its flight across the sky, then disappeared mysteriously into the western horizon. The golden crowns of Silla's shaman kings excavated in Kyongju all bear symbolic reindeer antlers which point up to heaven, reflecting the traditional role of Korean kings as high shaman priests. This rich symbolism, totally absent in the royal crowns of the west, was all derived from Korea's ancient shaman traditions.

The three primary goals of shaman ceremonies (*kut*) are to promote longevity, fertility and prosperity. Early in Korean history, Chinese Taoism, which also places great emphasis on longevity, strongly influenced Korean shamanism by providing practical techniques and advent of written history, have been completely assimilated by Korean artists and craftsmen. The national flag, for example, displays the cosmic *yin/yang* emblem and four trigrams drawn from the 3,000-year-old Chinese *Book of Changes* (*I-Ching*). The 12 animals of the Chinese zodiac are common motifs, as are the 'Three Friends of Winter' (pine, plum, and bamboo) and the 'Four Noble Gentlemen' (orchid, chrysanthemum, bamboo, and plum). Other symbols derived from

philosophical concepts to complement Korean traditions. It is interesting to note that the three cardinal Star Gods who appear in so many Chinese temples represent the same shaman goals of longevity, fertility and prosperity.

Shamanism was one of the earliest elements brought by Koreans to Japan, where it formed the basis for that country's 'native' Shinto religion. In fact, Shinto is traditional Korean shamanism painted with a thick Japanese veneer to mask its Korean origins.

Shaman traditions in Korea take two forms: symbolic expression in Korean art and ritual expression in Korean life. Indeed, Korean art motifs are impossible to appreciate without a basic knowledge of shamanist symbolism, specifically the Ten Symbols of Longevity, the Five Symbols which Repel Evil, and the Four Symbols of Good Luck. The Ten Symbols of Longevity are the *pullocho* (the magic mushroom of immortality), Turtle, Deer, Crane, Pine, Bamboo, Sun, Clouds, Rocks and Water.

The Turtle was often used as a massive base for the stone memorial steles commonly erected at the tombs of famous kings, monks, and other heroes in Korea. Cranes, the most popular of all Korean longevity symbols, still appear on everything from celadon teacups to embroidered pillow cases. Deer remain a popular art motif in painting, embroidery and other decorative arts, as do pine and bamboo. All these symbols frequently appear together on one of Korea's most common pieces of furniture: folding panel screens used as decorative room partitions.

The Five Symbols which repel evil are the Dragon, the Phoenix, the Tiger, the Turtle and the Ox. These symbols appear most often in homes, temples and public buildings to protect them from evil spirits. Shamans were even consulted in recent years by the Korean government to determine the most auspicious direction for the late President Park's gravesite, so that his spirit would derive maximum protection from the Tiger and the Dragon.

The Four Symbols of good luck are the Unicorn, the Turtle, the Phoenix and the Dragon. Unlike the unicorn of Western tradition, which resembles a horse, the Eastern unicorn has a dragon's head with a single horn, a deer's body and an ox's tail, thus combining attributes of several auspicious animals.

Chinese sources which commonly appear in Korean arts and crafts include the peach (long life), pomegranate (wealth), lotus (Buddhism), orchid (scholastic refinement), butterfly (romance), bat (happiness) and bamboo (resilience).

The basic arts and crafts of painting, calligraphy, architecture and ceramics first came to Korea from China and were later transmitted from Korea to Japan. This gives Korea a unique position in Oriental art history. It preserved and improved many forms of Chinese art and architecture which subsequently disappeared or degenerated in China, and it placed a permanent Korean stamp on the development of Japanese art and architecture. This pivotal position between China and Japan makes Korea a crucial source of information about the artistic traditions of both.

Music and Dance

Music and dance play central roles in Korean culture and remain the nation's most highly developed performing arts. Uniquely Korean styles of music and dance were first derived from shamanist ceremonies (*kut*) about 3,000 years ago. Today, music and dance are appreciated at all levels of Korean society and are performed in a great variety of styles, from the spontaneous efforts of inebriated amateurs dancing to the beat of chop-sticks and beer bottles to the highly skilled performances of professional dancers and musicians. Korean music is rich and vibrant, and improvisation plays a key role.

Shamanist music and dance traditions handed down from pre-historic Korea were taken up and continued during the Silla era by *hwarang* (Flower Youth), an exclusive knighthood of noble warriors selected for physical beauty, martial valour and artistic talent. During the Yi Dynasty (1392–1910), music and dance were sponsored by the royal court and became important elements in the repertoires of *kisaeng* (courtesans), who preserved many exotic forms that might otherwise have been lost. Music and dance were classified and given standard form, and court officials compiled a 'Book of Dance' as well as a 'Book of Music'.

Korean dance emphasizes inner feeling and mood, and much depends on the performer's inner inspiration. Rather than tell a story, a Korean dance strives to evoke a mood and convey feelings. The two key concepts are *hung* (inner feeling and mood) and *mut* (charm, grace, spiritual inspiration).

There are three major forms of Korean dance: court, religious, and folk. Traditional court dances were performed by male dancers and royal *kisaeng* for the entertainment of the royal family and their retinue. Common people never witnessed them. Two types were

distinguished: *hyang-ak* (Korean origin) and *tang-ak* (Chinese origin). While the steps were relatively simple, the costumes were highly elaborate and colourful. The most popular form was *Hwagwan-mu*, the Flower-Crown Dance, so named for the small sparkling crown worn by the performers. Religious dances were of three types: Shaman, Buddhist, and Confucian. Shaman dances, usually performed by female *mudang* (shamans), were central to *kut* (shaman ceremonies) and were used both to invoke spirits and to launch *mudang* into trance. Buddhist religious dances, some of which entered Korea from Central Asia, were used to supplicate Buddhist deities on behalf of departed souls to facilitate their journey to heaven. Confucian religious dances were highly ceremonial forms originally derived from China and authentically preserved in Korea. A classical Confucian dance may still be witnessed in all its classical pomp and pageantry twice a year (spring and autumn) at Sungkyunghwan University, and at the annual ceremonies commemorating Confucius' birth held at the Chongmyo Royal Shrine in Seoul.

The most quintessential Korean dances are the folk forms, which retain strong shamanist undertones. In Korean folk dance, the method of expressing inner emotions with outer motions is most apparent. Improvisation prevails over rote movement, and the rhythm constantly changes rather than following a fixed pattern. The oldest and most popular is the Farmer's Dance, in which performers spin madly about the stage to the urgent rhythms of drums and gongs. The Farmer's Dance is still performed as a shaman rite to purify dwellings, supplicate benevolent spirits and exorcise evil forces.

Korea's most distinctive folk dance is the mask-dance drama, which usually satirizes the romantic peccadillos of lecherous monks and wayward aristocrats. The vividly painted masks, which cover the entire face, are highly original and expressive. Made of wood, gourd, or *papier-mâché*, the masks were traditionally burned after each performance in the belief that they became contaminated by spirits. However, some old masks did survive, and still serve as models for contemporary mask-makers.

The two most expressively powerful folk dances are solo forms known as Sungmu and Salbu-ri. The Sungmu, or Buddhist Priest Dance, re-enacts the seduction of a famous monk by the renowned *kisaeng* Hwang Chin-I, who had a penchant for making celibates break their vows for a brief taste of her beauty. Performed with the right mood and inspiration, this can be the most expressive and emotionally moving of all Korean folk dances.

Korean music follows a five-note scale, which is why it often sounds

Shamanism Today

Shaman ceremonies (*kut*) are still performed regularly in Korea by shaman mediums (*mudang*), a role played primarily by women. In northern Korea, *mudang* are selected by divine calling, a rather chaotic process involving hallucinations, clairvoyance and highly eccentric behaviour which continues to torment the candidate until her divine powers are recognized. In the southern parts of the peninsula, *mudang* inherit their roles through family lineage and are trained for their calling from an early age.

Common reasons for women in Korea to summon a *mudang* to perform a *kut* in their homes include illness, husbands who squander family wealth on mistresses, marital squabbles, failure in business, burglaries and so forth. Other appropriate occasions for a *kut* are such momentous events as birth, marriage or death, blessing a new house, or invoking rain during a prolonged drought.

A *kut* lasts many hours, sometimes all night. First the woman of the house takes the *mudang* on a complete tour of her home to drive evil spirits from every nook and corner, while respectfully observing the benevolent spirits which reside in the kitchen, on the *kimchee* jars, along the roofbeams, behind the doors, and even in the outhouse. Then, with a colourful blend of music, dance and song, the *mudang* proceeds to purify the household and supplicate the gods. After conjuring up the spirits and working herself into a deep trance, she expresses the spirits' meanings in mime. Since a *mudang* in trance must commune with many different spirits and deities — both benevolent and malevolent — her behaviour can grow very wild and unpredictable, and the *kut* inevitably leaves her thoroughly exhausted.

The god most commonly supplicated during a shaman *kut* is the Roof-Beam Spirit or House God. If the House God is neglected for too long, he gets angry and stops protecting the house from evil, which brings untold calamity to the household. The *mudang* first exorcises the household of the evil demons to which the irate House God has deliberately given entry, then she placates the deity with incantations and offerings of food, wine, and cash. After the House God has gleaned the 'essence' from the food and wine, family and friends consume the 'gross' remains, while the *mudang* keeps the cash.

In Seoul, one can catch a *kut* at Kuksadong, a public shrine located just above Sajik Park. Sometimes several *kut* a day are performed there. On Tano Day, a traditional spring festival, colourful *kut* continue for a full week at the east coast town of Kangnung, about 3.5 hours from Seoul. In Seoul, Tano Day is celebrated on the banks of the Han River with elaborate shaman ceremonies in honour of the Dragon King.

Should you happen to be in the vicinity when a *kut* is in progress, it is worth getting up close to observe and even participate. Share the ritual offerings of food and wine and throw in a token offering of cash.

'out of tune' to Western ears accustomed to a seven-note scale. While there exists no systematic harmony in Korean music, melodies can be quite striking, with sudden shifts in rhythm and metre, bold runs, abrupt pauses and exquisite undertones. Among the most popular traditional instruments are the *changgo* (drum with hour-glass shape), *kayagum* (12-string zither with silk strings), *piri* (a shrill bamboo pipe with double-reed mouthpiece), *taegum* (bamboo flute), and chimes of both metal and stone. There are 12 official genres of Korean music, but the folk forms are by far the richest and most varied.

Another interesting art, which relies almost entirely on the performer's voice, is the *pansori*, a type of story-telling through dramatic song. Accompanied only by a barrel drum, the performer sings popular folk-tales in a strong, dramatic voice which conveys the mood as much as the meaning of the story.

Today, one sees Koreans performing traditional music and dance in public parks, at picnics, in the mountains, at beach resorts and in local taverns throughout the country. These spontaneous performances are usually fuelled with generous doses of *soju* spirits and occur frequently during holidays and festivals. Call the Korean Culture and Arts Foundation at 741-0500 or the Sejong Cultural Centre at 720-3671 to get a listing of professional shows.

Confucius, Buddha and Christ

Like that in China and Japan, religious life in Korea has been moulded mainly by the two great sages of Asia: Confucius and Buddha. Ancestor worship and other Confucian traditions became inextricably linked with Buddhist rituals in ancient China, and in Japan the Confucian code of ethics known as *bushido* influenced and was in turn influenced by the Japanese form of Buddhism known as Zen. Much the same was true in Korean religion, but in the 19th century a third great figure was introduced to Korea by Christian missionaries; of all the peoples of Asia, Koreans seem to have the strongest affinity for the teachings of Jesus Christ.

The ancient Chinese referred to Koreans as 'the ceremonious people of the East', in admiration of their strict Confucian etiquette. Korea's strict hierarchical social structure managed to absorb and institutionalize the conservative social ethics of Confucian philosophy in a way which China, with all her diversity and relative social mobility, has never done. This Confucian legacy is manifested daily in modern Korea. Men automatically pay deference to superiors and elders by standing up, bowing low, and pouring forth a stream of polite phrases; women automatically defer to men in public and still play second-fiddle at home; children pay homage to parents and teachers and everyone treats foreign visitors as honoured guests.

The virtues of politeness and propriety are so ingrained in Korean society that the government regularly broadcasts public service messages on commercial radio stations to teach Korean people polite phrases in English to use with foreign visitors. Courteous English expressions such as 'How do you do', 'Thank you very much', and 'Please visit Korea again' are common usage among contemporary Koreans. Western visitors seem to take this all for granted, but how many Americans or English greet Asian visitors to their shores using polite phrases in the visitor's native tongue? In Korea, Confucian etiquette demands it.

When Yi Song-gye — later known as Taejo, the 'Great Founder' — established the Yi Dynasty in Korea in 1392, Taejo and his Neo-Confucian advisors denounced Buddhist beliefs and practices as wasteful and superstitious, and severely restricted the power of the Buddhist clergy. Though Taejo's motives were largely political, his policies dealt a devastating blow to Buddhism's overall influence in Korea, which henceforth was restricted to the spiritual realm. Filial piety (a polite term for absolute obedience to elders) became the supreme social virtue, and ancestor worship became the primary religious ceremony in every household, supplanting Buddhist rites.

With its traditionally hierachical and ethnically uniform society, Korea took Confucius literally and implemented his conservative social precepts so effectively that they still guide and colour Korean social life today.

Neo-Confucian thought and teaching relegated women to the very bottom of the social strata. Their real function in society was to serve men as playmates and to bear male heirs. To this day, women in Korea do not adopt their husbands' surnames after marriage — not because of women's liberation but because the social status of women is so low that they are not deemed worthy of carrying a man's family name. Until recently girls received no formal education and were confined to their family home before marriage and their husband's home afterwards. One reason for the great popularity of the jumping see-saw game among women of old Korea was that it afforded them a few brief glimpses of the world beyond the courtyard walls. The only women with any access to public life and personal freedom in Korea were *kisaeng*, who from the age of 15 to 30 enjoyed colourful, sophisticated life-styles and earned both money and fame from powerful patrons throughout the kingdom. *Kisaeng* were the only women permitted a proper education, for intelligence and talent were essential assets in their profession. But unlike Chinese 'sing-song girls' and Japanese *geisha*, Korea's *kisaeng* were prohibited from marrying their wealthy patrons. After their efflorescence faded, they were treated as outcasts and many became Buddhist nuns.

Today, Korean women play relatively active roles in public life, although at home they still adopt the traditional role of deference toward their husbands. Women hold important positions in government and form 'the power behind the throne' in many corporations. Yet despite their newfound freedom, contemporary Korean women still cultivate traditional feminine charms in order to soothe and subdue the volatile male ego.

Buddhism came to Korea from China during the late fourth century AD, and for 1,000 years it remained the dominant cultural force throughout the Land of Morning Calm, enjoying the same power and prestige as Christianity did during the Middle Ages in Europe. Buddhism inspired Korea's art, architecture, and literature. Even after Confucius replaced Buddha as the official state sage in 1392, Buddha remained the people's primary spiritual guide.

Buddhism's greatest period of acceptance in Korea occurred during the Koryo Dynasty (935–1392), when Buddhist priests wielded enormous power at the royal court. The third son of every family was required by law to enter the priesthood, and over 80,000 temples were in active operation throughout the kingdom. Again, this period also saw the completion of the Tripitaka Koreana, a mammoth 19-year labour of faith in which the complete original Chinese translation of the Buddhist scriptures was engraved on 80,000 wooden tablets, still stored in an ancient library at the Haein Temple in central Korea.

Korean Buddhism is highly 'ecumenical', and all schools of Buddhist thought are taught and respected. Amitabha Buddha, Sakyamuni Buddha, Maitreya (the Buddha of the Future) and Guanyin (the Buddha of Mercy and Compassion) are the most revered deities. Most large temples maintain icons and shrinehalls for all four.

Buddhist art and architecture reached a zenith in Korea. While the basic style and colour schemes of Korean temples were first adopted from Tang China, Korean craftsmen further embellished and improved Chinese models with local lore and superior materials. Korean envoys later transmitted these revised Chinese models to Japan, where they remain the standard for Japanese temple construction to this day.

Koreans became especially adept at building stone pagodas. The kingdom's rugged mountains provided abundant supplies of high-quality granite, a favourite material for Korean artisans, and with it they fashioned thousands of multi-tiered pagodas which still grace the countryside. Indeed, Korea is also known as the 'Land of Stone Pagodas'. The most famous pair of pagodas date from AD 750 and stand in the main courtyard of Pulguk-sa in Kyongju.

The most sublimely beautiful, aesthetically perfect work of Buddhist art in Korea — perhaps in the entire world — is the sculptured image of Sakyamuni at the Sokkuram Cave Grotto in Kyongju.

Today there are about 14 million practising Buddhists and 2,500 active temples throughout Korea, which makes Buddhism the nation's most popular faith. The two major sects are T'aego, which permits marriage among its clergy and currently counts 2,500 monks and 300 nuns nationwide, and the dominant Chogye sect, which demands celibacy among its 8,000 monks and 5,000 nuns. If you happen to be in Korea on Buddha's Birthday (the eighth day of the fourth lunar month, usually mid-May), it is well worth spending the day in a Buddhist temple. There you will witness the living tradition of Buddhism played out with the same colourful pageantry and elaborate rituals that have sustained it in Korea for over 1,600 years.

Among the first things one notices in Seoul, Pusan, Taegu and other Korean cities are the steeples of Christian churches etched against the skyline. Indeed some observers have dubbed Seoul 'the city of churches'. Despite severe persecutions suffered by Christians when the faith was first introduced during the 19th century, Christianity has gained a surprisingly firm foothold in the Hermit Kingdom, and today

the Christian Bible is the second most widely read book in the nation after the Chinese classic *Romance of the Three Kingdoms.*
Ironically, the first Western Christian missionary to set foot in Korea came with the Japanese invasion forces sent by Hideyoshi in 1592. He was a Spanish Jesuit named Gregorio de Cespedes, and he accompanied General Konishi, a Christian convert in command of the Japanese Christian troops sent to spearhead the invasion of Korea.

In 1795, a Chinese Catholic priest named James Chu entered Korea from Beijing and began to preach the Christian faith, but he was soon executed as a subversive. Due to mounting pressures from conservative Confucian ministers at court, repression against Christians in Korea continued to grow throughout the 19th century, culminating in the bloody pogroms of 1866, when nine of the 12 French Catholic missionaries residing in Korea were publicly beheaded on the banks of the Han River in Seoul. Over the next three years, 8,000 of Korea's 11,000 Christian converts were ruthlessly massacred. Today, the Church of the Martyrs stands on the spot along the Han River where the priests lost their heads, and on the second floor is a museum of relics and a memorial dedicated to them and their martyred converts.

In 1882, a formal protocol was signed by Korea and the U.S.A., establishing diplomatic relations and providing for the protection of Western missionaries working in Korea. Thereafter, missionaries of the various Protestant sects joined the Catholic effort in Korea and Christianity began to flourish.

During the brutal Japanese occupation of Korea (1910–45), Christian missionaries actively encouraged Korean resistance, which placed the Christian church in a highly favourable light in patriotic Korean eyes. Christians also established educational institutions for women — unprecedented in old Korea — and this further enhanced the church's appeal to the women of the country. However, this tradition of social activism has also led Korean church leaders into trouble from time to time, especially in recent years, when Christian activists have become embroiled in opposition politics. Nevertheless, Christianity remains a vibrant force in Korean national life, and its influence continues to grow.

Today, there are about nine million Christians in Korea (1.5 million Catholics and 7.5 million Protestants). This represents about 20 percent of the population and indicates a growing rate of conversion, especially among Korea's national leaders and intellectual elite. Christians in Korea form an active, powerful minority which continues to raise the Christian cross atop new church steeples on the horizons of the Land of Morning Calm and forges one of the country's closest links with the Western world.

Korean Cuisine

If indeed you are what you eat, then the dynamic energy and drive of the Korean people might well be traced to their diet. The least known of Asia's great culinary traditions, Korean cuisine is fundamentally different from that of both China and Japan.

Koreans eat three full meals a day, the number of dishes increasing with each meal. At least half a dozen dishes appear with a traditional Korean breakfast, twice as many with lunch, and up to 20 or more with a complete dinner banquet. Short-grain rice is the staple at every meal, and today it is usually blended with barley or millet to stretch limited rice supplies, also providing added nutritional value. Like the Chinese and Japanese, Koreans eat noodles, beancurd, bean sprouts and lentils. But here the similarity ends.

The most popular methods of cooking in Korea are in communal hot-pots and by grilling meat over charcoal or gas braziers. Both reflect early Mongol influences, and permit diners to cook their own food at the table. Traditionally, diners sat on cushions on *ondol* floors around low lacquered tables, and most Korean restaurants still have a few *ondol* rooms available alongside more contemporary table-and-chair dining rooms.

The hallmark of Korean cuisine is *kimchee*, a term which denotes any side-dish pickled in brine with garlic and chillis. It is an old Korean saying that 'a man can live without a wife, but not without *kimchee*'. And it is virtually impossible to find a Korean house, apartment or other dwelling without rows of big, black, enamelled *kimchee* pots fermenting away in the back yard, porch or on the balcony. 'As Korean as *kimchee*' is a common expression.

Chilli and garlic are the mainstays of the basic *kimchee* formula, which calls for heads of fresh cabbage to be cut open, salted, placed in brine with loads of chilli and garlic and set to ferment in big ceramic pots. In summer, when fermentation is rapid, *kimchee* is made fresh daily; in winter, the big *kimchee* pots are packed in straw and buried to their necks in the ground to prevent freezing, then left to ferment for months. Among the most popular varieties of this most typical of Korean dishes are *sobaegi kimchee:* cabbage stuffed with oysters; *oee sobaegi kimchee:* sliced cucumbers with radish and ginger; *kakdooki kimchee:* diced white radish with scallions and *dong chimi kimchee:* white radish sticks floating in brine.

Besides garlic and chilli, favourite Korean seasonings include scallions, ginger, sesame oil, sesame seeds, wine and soy sauce. Cooking herbs, which are applied according to the principles of traditional herbal medicine, include wild aster, aralia root, royal fern bracken, shepherd's purse, mugwort and bluebell. There is also a wide range of fermented pastes and sauces for dipping called *chang*. Every restaurant and home has its own formula for making *chang*, and each batch comes out different. Based on a fermented mash of soy beans, the three most common varieties are *kan chang* (a dark liquid, like soy sauce), *daen chang* (a thick, pungent paste) and *kochu chang* (a fiery version laced with chillis).

Rice is called *pap*, and soup is *kuk* or *tang*. *Panchan* is a category of side dishes which are neither *kimchee* nor main courses. *Panchan* provide a great variety of flavours and ingredients, balancing not only the culinary appeal but also the nutritional value of a meal. Popular gourmet *panchan*, many of which are also commonly consumed in taverns as *anju* (drinking snacks) include such treats as: *tubu:* soybean curd; *keechang:* raw crab legs marinated in fiery red-chilli sauce; *saengsun hwae:* sliced raw fish, or 'sashimi'; *myong nan jhot:* fish roe in garlic sauce; *sigumchi namul:* blanched spinach dressed with sesame oil and seeds; *myul chee chorim:* dried anchovies sautéed with chilli peppers; *saengsun yangyum:* broiled fish sprinkled with sesame seeds; *manul changah-chee:* green garlic pickled in soy sauce; *kul chun:* sautéed oysters; *don chun:* beef and bean-curd patties spiced with ginger; *pindaedok:* mung-bean pancake laced with shrimp; and *sabsamchock:* ground beef patties with garlic and sesame seeds.

Beef is the star of gourmet Korean cuisine, and Korea produces some of the tastiest, most tender beef in the world. *Bulgogi* (finely sliced beef) and *kalbi* (beef short-ribs) are the most popular. They are first marinated in soy sauce, wine, sugar and fragrant spices, then grilled at one's table on charcoal or gas braziers. For *kalbi*, a small grill is placed over the coals; for *bulgogi*, a round metal dome (inspired by the ancient Mongol warriors' helmet) with a moat around the edge to catch the juices is placed over the fire.

Another popular form of beef cookery is done on a heavy metal griddle, upon which diced beef and fresh vegetables are sautéed in front of you. Known more commonly throughout the world by its Japanese name, *teppanyaki* (iron-plate cooking) it is, in fact, an original Korean form of cookery.

For simpler meals — especially summer lunches — you could try one of the great Korean single-bowl meals. The most renowned is *naeng myon:* noodles of buckwheat or potato flour in cold broth, with sliced cucumber, pear-apple and pressed beef, topped with an egg and accompanied by choice of seasonings. Other popular Korean noodle meals include *momil kooksoo:* buckwheat noodles with sweet radish sauce; *odaeng kooksoo:* wheat noodles with fishcake in broth; *kong kooksoo:* wheat noodles in fresh soybean milk; *chap chae:* thin rice

(Left) Eating pancakes and drinking makkolli *at the Korean Folk Village.*

(Top Right) Rolled sushi, Korean-style.

noodles sautéed with meat and vegetables; and *udong:* broad wheat noodles with onions, beancurd, egg and chilli.

If rice is the choice, one could ask for *hanjongshik*, which literally means the meal of the day. This consists of a bowl of rice served with an array of side-dishes and a bowl of pickled cabbage soup. *Kongnamul pap* is a bit fancier, with bean sprouts, beef and spinach served over rice. The king of Korean rice dishes, however, is *pi pim pap*, which is as much fun to pronounce as to eat. A big bowl of rice is topped with bean sprouts, bluebell root, blanched fern bracken, spinach and a fried egg sunny-side up, accompanied with a bowl of soup, mixed with spoon and eaten with chopsticks.

One of the best single-bowl meals is *samgyae tang*, which consists of a whole spring chicken stuffed with rice, white ginseng and dried jujubes (Chinese dates), then steamed in its own broth in a heavy iron pot. This is also Korea's best example of the great Asian culinary tradition of blending food with medicine. Ginseng chicken soup is delicious and provides a potent tonic.

There are two dishes, formerly reserved exclusively for Korean royalty, which dedicated gourmets will certainly wish to try. *Kujolpan* (Nine Treasure Dish) comes in an octagonal lacquered dish with nine compartments. Delicate crêpes lie in the centre compartment, surrounded by the other eight treasures to be eaten in the crêpes: shredded egg, sautéed cucumbers, onions, mushrooms, beef, carrots, cabbage and shrimps.

The other royal delicacy of Korea is *sinsunlo*, which comes in a brass pot with a chimney, much like a Mongolian fire-pot. Sliced beef with chopped onions and seasonings are placed in the bottom, with eggs, carrots, cucumbers, beef liver, chopped beef, blanched walnuts and fried gingko nuts neatly arranged on top. Live coals are then dropped into the chimney, while hot broth is poured over the ingredients. After being simmered briefly but well, this rich, royal fare is ready to eat.

A variety of delicious teas are usually served with traditional Korean cuisine, but not from the tea plant (*Camellia sinensis*), as in China and Japan. Koreans prefer teas brewed from grains, dried fruits, and ginseng. *Bori cha* (barley tea) is the national beverage and is served free of charge at every restaurant, café, and tearoom in the country. *Moque cha* (quince tea) and *hodo cha* (walnut tea) are other common varieties. *Insam cha* (ginseng tea) is a popular tonic drunk year-round by Koreans of all ages and walks of life. In recent years, *kopi* (coffee) has also become a popular drink in Korea.

Korean Liquors and Drinking Habits

Drinking has always played an important role in Korean leisure life, especially at the king's court. Many of the oldest ceramics excavated in Korea are drinking cups and liquor vessels, and there are many references to drinking parties in traditional Korean literature and painting.

Formerly, only men attended drinking parties. Other than professional *kisaeng*, who often matched their guests cup for cup, women never drank in public. That tradition is definitely changing, for the women of contemporary Korea seem to be just as fond of liquor as Korean men.

Indeed, drinking is almost a national pastime today, and there is no better way for a foreign visitor to delve beneath the veneer of ceremonial courtesy and get to know Korean character than by drinking with Koreans in a typical Korean *sul-jup* (liquor house).

However, certain elements of traditional Korean drinking etiquette are still observed among Koreans, especially at major banquets. Foreigners who display a familiarity with these traditions inevitably impress their Korean hosts. For one thing, you raise your glass to your lips only when proposing or accepting a toast. If you are the thirsty type, then exercise your imagination to think up new toasts. For an extra measure of traditional courtesy, raise your glass with two hands when toasting and drinking. It is acceptable practice to drink oneself into oblivion at Korean banquets and *kisaeng* parties, for there is no stigma attached to drunken revelry in Korea.

The most popular native Korean liquors are *soju:* a distillate of sweet potatoes — the least expensive and most potent Korean liquor which, if taken in excess, leaves a nasty hangover; *makkolli:* a milky white brew fermented from rice and reputed to be highly nutritious, and is Korea's most popular native liquor; *popchu:* a high-grade rice wine similar to Japanese *sake* and usually served hot, a speciality of Konju; *insam-ju:* ginseng liquor made by immersing an entire ginseng root in clear rice wine (the best brand is 'Jinro', drunk as a tonic); and *paem-sool:* another potent tonic liquor, made by immersing an entire snake in strong spirits.

Beer (*maekju*) is rapidly becoming a popular drink in Korea, where there are two local brands. 'OB' (Oriental Brewery) is considered the best, followed by 'Crown' bottled beer (*pyong-maekju*), available at almost every restaurant, roadside stall, café and teahouse. Draught beer (*saeng-maekju*) is served in beer-halls, which specialize in this beverage; it is also served in many Western hotels and restaurants. Another type of beer-hall is called *tong-dalk-jip*, an establishment

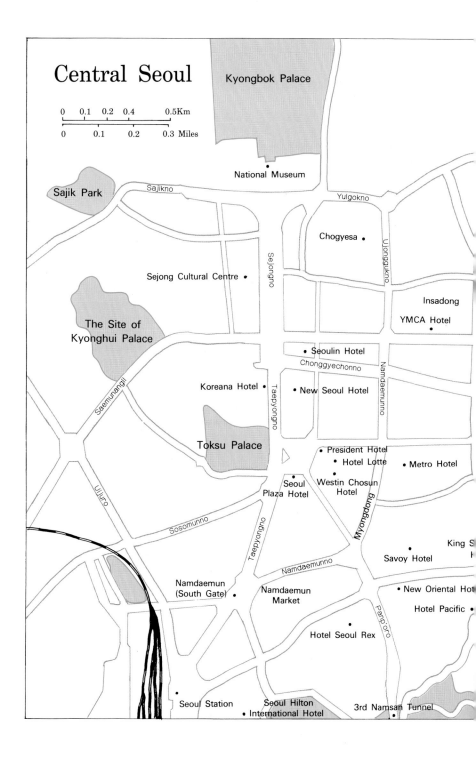

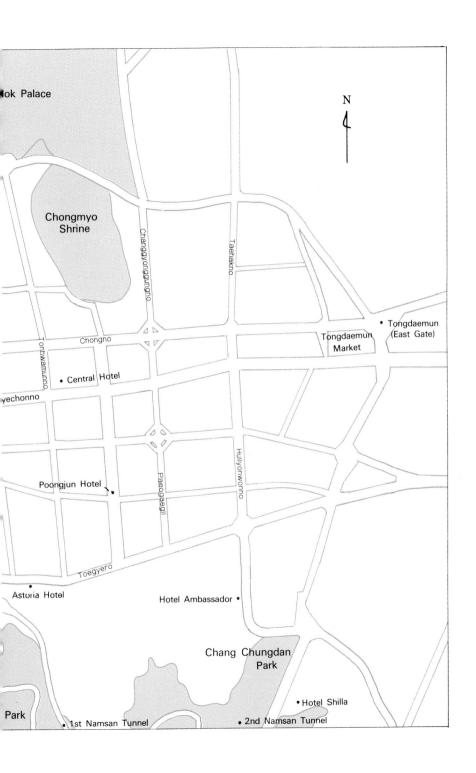

which specializes in broiled chicken and draught beer.

Yang-ju (foreign liquor) is also growing in popularity, especially in Seoul. Imported foreign liquors are heavily taxed and therefore highly priced. Korea now produces its own whisky, gin, brandy and other Western liquors, using imported ingredients and technology. There are currently three whiskies distilled in Korea, all from imported malts, the best of which is a surprisingly smooth, very tasty blend called 'Blackstone', made in co-operation with Chivas Regal. A few Western-style grape wines are also on the market, the most palatable being a Riesling wine which appears under the 'Ma-ju-ang' label. Most hotels, Western restaurants and liquor shops stock it.

Koreans never drink without *anju* (drinking snacks) to munch on. *Anju* serve dual (and somewhat contradictory) purposes. They protect the stomach by absorbing potent spirits and, at the same time, create a thirst for more liquor. Whether you go to a *sul-jip* (liquor house) to drink or a *sik-tang* (restaurant) to eat, food and liquor are inevitably consumed together.

Seoul

Seoul means 'capital' in Korean and has served as Korea's political and cultural centre since 1392, when King Taejong established the capital of the Yi Dynasty at the place then called Hanyang. The old city was originally protected by a 16-kilometre (ten-mile) stone wall with nine gates, five of which have been restored as national monuments. Today, however, Seoul sprawls well beyond its original city limits.

The old and the new exist side by side in Seoul. The graceful, curving eaves of ancient palaces, temples and shrines — all faithfully restored to their original splendour — are seen between the glass walls of modern high-rises. Businessmen in stylish Western business suits stroll along the boulevards with wives dressed in *hanbok*, the traditional billowy garb of pastel silk and satin worn by Korean women since ancient times. Even men and women with modern university educations still submit to marriages arranged by their parents in the classical Confucian tradition. *Kimchee* is chased down with gulps of chilled Coca-Cola, and even ginseng — Korea's most ancient panacea — takes modern form in instant tea, shampoo and chewing gum.

Moreover, Seoul sits only 56 kilometres (35 miles) from one of the world's most hostile and heavily armed borders. The constant threat of communist aggression from the north has strengthened Seoul's determination to preserve its hard-won freedom and precious cultural heritage.

Seoul is a vibrant, exuberant city, full of high hopes and replete with energy to achieve them. The dynamic spirit of Seoul is well reflected in the city's preparations for the 1988 Olympic Games. Heavy construction, including a massive expansion of the subway system, has completely transformed the face of the city for this event.

Koreans have a marvellous ability to balance the requirements of business and pleasure. Nowhere is this more evident than in the *tabang* (tearooms) which abound throughout Seoul. *Tabang* serve coffee, tea and soft drinks at minimal prices in a cosy, softly lit atmosphere. Some even provide live music, and all are equipped with excellent sound systems. You may sit for hours in the intimate ambience of a *tabang* without pressure from the house to spend a lot of money. The *tabang* is as much a social as a commercial institution, a casual oasis where one may conduct business or simply relax away from sterile offices and crowded city streets.

The most distinctive landmark in Seoul is the Namsan Tower, perched high on Nam (South) San (Mountain). Three major tunnels run through Namsan, which sits near the southern edge of the old city limits. The central business district, which may be easily reached by

directing your driver to the Chosun or Lotte Hotels, is only a few steps from City Hall, the elegant old Toksu Palace, and the bustling Myong-dong shopping and pleasure district. To browse in the shops or visit the bars of Seoul's most colourful nightlife district, simply ask for 'Itaewon'. And to reach the markets of eastern Seoul, as well as the Seoul Stadium, with all its neighbourhood sporting goods shops, the key word is 'Tongdaemun', the Great East Gate. Remember also that regardless of where you're going in Seoul, traffic will be congested. Patience is always required when visiting the city.

City Sights

Seoul is one of those rare cities that does not always put commerce before culture. Despite the fast pace of modern development, the government has decreed that all architectural and other cultural relics in Seoul must be preserved and protected for posterity. Consequently, the city is full of interesting historical sights. Since modern Seoul was superimposed upon the old city, these sights are often located in incongruous settings and surrounded by snarling traffic. However, once inside their ancient walls, you can feel you are entering another world.

Toksu Palace

Located in the heart of the city, across the street from the Seoul Plaza Hotel, the Toksu Palace once served as the royal residence of Prince Daegon, elder brother of King Songjong (reigned 1470–98) of the Yi Dynasty. It was also used as a residence by King Kojung, one of Korea's last monarchs, before the Japanese forced him to abdicate in 1907.

Toksu Palace was built about the same time as Beijing's Forbidden City, and the influence of classical Chinese architecture can be clearly seen here, although the Koreans' influence is equally evident. The palace's famous peony gardens draw thousands of visitors every spring.

A Neo-Palladian style building, designed by a British architect at the turn of the century, provides an architectural surprise among the Oriental eaves of the Toksu Palace grounds. It currently houses Korea's National Museum of Modern Art.

Kyongbok Palace and the National Museum

The Palace of Shining Happiness was built in 1394 by Taejo, founder of the Yi (Chosun) Dynasty, when he moved the kingdom's capital to Hanyang (Seoul). It was burned to ashes by the Japanese during their

invasion in 1592, rebuilt between 1865 and 1869, then destroyed again by the Japanese during their 20th-century campaign to eradicate Korean culture. Of the original 330 structures, only ten major buildings survive today.

Of central interest here is a ten-storey pagoda dating from the ancient Koryo Kingdom nearly 2,000 years ago. Other pagodas and national monuments have also been moved to the Kyongbok Palace grounds during the past decades in order to fill the empty spaces left by demolished buildings. Korea's National Museum, which contains artefacts from all three kingdoms (Koryo, Paekche and Silla), as well as all subsequent dynasties (Silla, Koryo and Yi), is housed in a spacious, regal building within the palace grounds. In its uncluttered corridors and quiet alcoves you may view the fruits of 5,000 years of Korean civilization.

The restored buildings of the Kyongbok Palace give excellent impressions of classical Korean architecture at its best. Among the elegant structures here is the quiet pavilion where King Sejong conceived *hangul*, the Korean alphabet. The Hall of Happy Meetings, an enormous open banquet pavilion set amid an artifical lake, is still used occasionally by the Korean government to throw lavish welcome receptions for visiting foreign dignitaries. The entire palace complex is laced with numerous garden-grottos and landscaped with lovely lotus ponds.

The Kyongbok Palace is Seoul's 'Forbidden City', built a full century before Beijing's and no doubt was magnificent prior to its destruction by Japanese invaders. Kyongbok reflects a far more human spirit and earthly orientation than do the palaces of Beijing's Forbidden City. The atmosphere appears less contrived and the style less pretentious than that of Chinese imperial architecture. Korean architecture celebrates the harmony of man and nature, incorporating flowers, trees, birds and bees with the culturally contrived designs of man.

Changdok Palace and the Secret Garden

If you visit only one historical site in Seoul, then the Palace of Shining Virtue with its exquisite Secret Garden is the place to go. It was built in 1405 by the third king of Chosun (Yi) to serve as a second palace in the new capital. Also destroyed by the Japanese in 1592, it has been restored several times since, and is Seoul's best-preserved palace and the city's most popular tourist attraction.

Once again, the harmonious balance between heaven and earth, man and nature, *yin* and *yang* — so well depicted on the Korean national flag — is everywhere reflected in the architecture and gardens of the Changdok Palace. Note that all the buildings except one display the distinctive dragon ridge of piled tiles which runs along the main axis of the roofs. The sole exception was the king's personal sleeping quarters. Since the king was the living personification of the dragon, his quarters required no special dragon ridge for protection.

Another distinctive feature of Korean architecture here is the tall, narrow brick chimneys standing adjacent to each building. These were used to ventilate the underground fires which kept the palace's *ondol* floors warm during the cold winter months.

A delicate 400-year old plum tree, a gift from the emperor of Ming China to King Sonjo (reigned 1568–1608), still grows in the palace grounds. How it survived the repeated ravages of fire and war in Korean history is hard to imagine.

Through a gate behind the palace grounds one enters the famous Secret Garden, surely one of the most beautiful court gardens in the world. Every feature, from walls and walkways, ponds and pavilions, to the shady groves and flowering gardens of this tranquil 31-hectare (78-acre) garden retreat, has been faithfully restored to its original state. The entire garden is alive with pheasants, magpies and other birdlife.

Of particular interest is the Yongkyongdong House, a perfectly preserved example of a classical Korean gentry home, located in the heart of the Secret Garden. This unusual architectural relic dates from 1828, when the king ordered an exact replica of a typical home of the gentry to be built there for his own use. Occasionally, the king would retire to this house, don simple country clothing, eat simple country food, and emulate the rustic life of a rural gentleman for a few days.

Tourists may enter the Changdok Palace and Secret Garden only in guided groups, which start at regular intervals from the main gate and are conducted in English, Chinese, Japanese and Korean.

Chongmyo Shrine

The Chongmyo Shrine lies in a secluded garden southeast of the Changdok Palace and houses the ancestral tablets of Yi-Dynasty kings and queens. Tourists may wander about and enjoy the beauties of the thickly forested grounds, but the two courtyards and main shrinehall are kept closed except for ceremonies on certain holidays.

One of those holidays occurs annually on the first Sunday in May, when a colourful Confucian ceremony is held to honour the spirits of Korea's royal ancestors. Celebrants dressed in elaborate traditional costumes pay homage to ancestral spirits with offerings of food and wine, and the exotic court music of ancient Korea is played on reed-pipe flutes, stone chimes, heavy drums, wooden clappers and other ancient instruments.

Namsan and the Pugak Skyway

Namsan, or South Mountain, with its needle-tipped tower on top, is Seoul's most conspicuous landmark. Surrounding this hilltop aerie is a spacious and beautifully landscaped park. The drive up and around Namsan is especially lovely in spring, when cherry blossoms, forsythia and azalea burst into colourful bloom, and in the autumn, when the trees turn flaming gold and red. Formerly closed to the public for security reasons, the tower is now open for sightseeing. The restaurant at the top of the tower offers marvellous views of the city.

Opposite Namsan is the Pugak Skyway, which runs along the crest of Seoul's northern hills. No pedestrian traffic is permitted on the Pugak Skyway, so you'll have to visit by private car or tour bus. At the top is the Sky House, which has a bar and restaurant for refreshment and affords sweeping views of Seoul from the opposite perspective of Namsan. Here you can also see remnant portions of the old wall which protected the city from attack, a miniature 'Great Wall of Korea'.

Chogye Temple

The only important temple located within Seoul's city limits, the Chogye Temple is headquarters of Korea's official Chogye sect of Buddhism and the administrative centre of 1,500 affiliated temples throughout the country. Located downtown near the Gukdong Building, it is readily accessible from any hotel.

Though the temple is always colourful and humming with activity, by far the best time to visit Chogye-sa (*sa* means temple) is on Buddha's Birthday, which falls on the eighth day of the fourth lunar month (usually early or mid-May). This auspicious event is celebrated with great fanfare at Chogye-sa and other Buddhist temples throughout Korea. The faithful purchase paper lanterns to which they attach long streamers inscribed with the names of their family members, and these are hung by the hundreds throughout the temple grounds. As evening falls, worshippers light little candles inside the lanterns and chant prayers for the year to come.

Many foreign residents of Seoul participate in this annual celebration by purchasing and hanging paper lanterns of their own to ensure good luck for themselves and their families during the coming year. The cost, a contribution to the temple, runs to about W10,000.

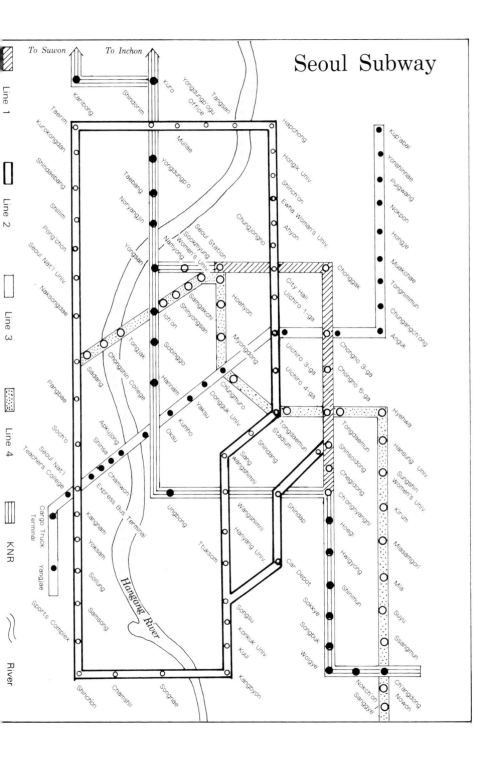

Cultural Centres

For Korean culture 'at a glance', you may visit the government-sponsored **Korea House**, located near the northern slopes of Namsan. Set in an oriental garden, the traditionally styled Korea House offers free Korean folk dance performances every Saturday and Sunday at 3 pm. In addition, there is a nightly programme of stage entertainment which includes traditional Korean song and dance, shaman rituals, mask-dance drama, solos on classical instruments, and other performances. Cultural films may be viewed upon request, and a tourist concession counter sells English-language books on every aspect of Korean culture and society. A restaurant inside serves traditional Korean cuisine.

The **Sejong Cultural Centre**, centrally located within view of the capitol building, was completed in 1978 and blends the beauty of traditional Korean style with the scale and functional design of modern architecture. It boasts a 99-rank organ, one of few in Asia, and the entire complex forms a true marvel of elegance and acoustics. Symphonies, plays, ballets and other cultural activities are frequently held here and at the National Theatre, featuring both renowned Korean and foreign talents.

The Olympic Stadiums

Koreans have always been keenly interested in sports, and take great pride in the fact that Seoul was selected to host the 1988 Olympics — the second Asian nation to hold this honour (Japan was host in 1964). To accommodate this huge event, the government spent US$170 million to construct the Seoul Sports Complex, the Olympic Park, the Olympic Village and the Press Village, all located east of the city, across the Han River.

The Seoul Sports Complex covers an area of 545,000 square metres (654,000 square yards) and includes two gymnasiums, an indoor Olympic pool, the Olympic Stadium, a baseball park and a warm-up field. The Olympic Stadium occupies 132,000 square metres (158,000 square yards) of floorspace and can accommodate 100,000 spectators. The Olympic Park is located four kilometres (2.5 miles) from the main complex, with a park and athletic facilities that cover a total of 2.9 million square metres (3.1 million square yards). This park is also full of interesting historical sites and is well worth a visit.

Youido

Another modern sight of interest in Seoul is Youido, a small island in the Han River, across from the Mapodaegyo Bridge. Known as the

'Manhattan of Seoul', this once deserted wasteland has been transformed into one of Seoul's major metropolitan hubs and the city's biggest showcase of modern architecture. Here one will find the National Assembly building, corporate headquarters of Korea's biggest companies, the Korea Stock Exchange, and the tallest building in Asia — the towering Daehan Life Insurance Building, known as DLI63. This building has an excellent observation deck on top, the Sea World aquarium, a roof garden, and the Imax Theatre. Youido Plaza is a huge public concourse used for military parades, public receptions for visiting dignitaries (Pope John Paul II visited in 1984), and other outdoor gatherings.

Shopping

Seoul is a shopper's paradise. Whether you are in the market for such traditional Korean products as antique chests, celadon, silk and ginseng, or such popular contemporary items as ready-made fashion wear, calculators, watches and sports accessories, Seoul offers a wide range of high-quality products at reasonable prices.

There are many interesting shopping districts in Seoul, and each area tends to specialize in certain types of products, although arcades and department stores usually offer a little of everything.

Popular Products

Korea's most famous product is **ginseng**, the mysterious man-root which has been used medicinally for thousands of years in Korea and China. Since ginseng production is a state monopoly, prices are fixed nationwide. You can shop for this 'magical' herb at any department store, arcade shop, duty-free outlet or other licensed concession.

Silk is another renowned product of Korea, and experienced fabric shoppers will immediately recognize the great bargains to be found of this precious material in Seoul. Today many American department stores buy finished silk products wholesale in Korea. Even Thailand imports considerable quantities of raw silk from Korea to make its famous 'Thai Silk' products. If the proprietor indicates that his product is pure silk, the shopper should be satisfied that it is not synthetic or mixed-fibre fabric, which sells for considerably less. The latter variety is also very beautifully made and remains popular throughout the world. Seoul's biggest selection of silk in bulk is found in the Tongdaemun Market. Don't be afraid to haggle over prices there. Far from offending the vendor, you will earn his respect. For ready-made

silk clothing, the boutiques of Myong-dong and hotel arcades are good places to shop.

Korean **ceramics** are prized throughout the world for craftsmanship and originality of design. Celadon, with its distinctive blue-green glaze and white inlaid designs, is by far the most famous product of Korean kilns. Today, Korean craftsmen turn out excellent reproductions of renowned Koryo celadon, delicate Yi-Dynasty white porcelain and earthy Silla ceramics. The most popular items are stemmed wine cups and long-necked wine decanters, teacups and teapots, incense burners, vases and decorative bowls. The best shopping district for ceramics is Insadong, although every shopping arcade and department store in Seoul also offers selections of high-quality ceramics. Be forewarned that blue-green celadon is expensive everywhere in Korea because about 90 percent of all production is deliberately destroyed due to minor flaws and imperfections. This practice ensures that every item on the market meets the highest standards of quality.

Korean **antiques**, especially medicine cabinets and clothing chests, are prized by collectors everywhere. The best — and most expensive — are to be found in the shops of Insadong, where antique chests, furniture and fixtures are on display in great variety. Koreans generally shop for antiques in Cheong-Gye Chil-ga, where hard bargaining often leads to prize purchases. Foreigners should take along a Korean friend or guide to overcome the language barrier. In Itaewon there are shops which sell original antiques as well as excellent reproductions at reasonable prices. While Itaewon does not offer the best quality of antiques in Seoul, it certainly offers the best prices, and for reproductions it is definitely the best place to shop. Sometimes it is better to buy reproductions because genuine antiques must be cleared for export with a certificate from the Cultural Property Preservation Bureau, and this can be a lengthy process. When buying rare antiques, always be sure to ask the dealer whether or not the item is exportable, otherwise you may have to leave it in Korea.

For **contemporary clothing** and **consumer products**, Seoul provides a dazzling display of choice. In Itaewon you can buy the same shirts, sweaters, jackets and pants exported to, and sold in, American department stores for about one-third the American price. Watches, calculators and lighters are sold in arcades and department stores throughout the city. For stylish contemporary fashions, the boutiques of Myong-dong and hotel arcades offer a wide range of high-quality wear at prices which compare favourably with similar shops in the West.

Other items to look for while shopping in Seoul include lacquerware inlaid with mother-of-pearl, brassware, embroidered

Korean quilt-covers, bedspreads, pillow-cases, bamboo, woven-straw products, amethyst, smokey topaz, leather and eelskin clothing, and wood carvings.

Shopping Districts

Seoul's shopping districts are easy to find, although the sheer number of shops and products can often be confusing. If you show your passport upon purchase, you will be exempt from all local sales taxes. The best way to shop in Seoul is to select one or two districts per day and cover them thoroughly. There are restaurants, snack stalls, coffee shops and beer halls in and around every shopping district, so take time along the way to pause for refreshment as you browse in the following districts:

Myong-dong Located in the heart of downtown Seoul, Myong-dong is Seoul's busiest district and its centre of high fashion. Bustling from morning until midnight, Myong-dong is a maze of narrow lanes full of fashion boutiques, silk shops, shoe stores and custom tailors, as well as Korean, Japanese and Chinese restaurants, coffee shops, *tabang*, bars, salons and beer-halls.

Insadong Sometimes called 'Mary's Alley' by foreigners, Insadong is located not far from the Chogye Temple. The street is lined with art galleries and antique shops, as well as stores specializing in Korean furniture, celadon and white porcelain, wood carving, scrolls, paintings, and beautifully embroidered Korean quilt covers, bedspreads and pillow cases, both in silk and synthetics. Korean pillow cases make especially nice gifts for friends back home because they are easy to carry, inexpensive, and typically Korean in design. Insadong boasts the highest quality as well as the highest prices for antiques in Seoul. Especially attractive are old Korean herbal medicine cabinets, clothing chests and antique cosmetic cases complete with mirror and miniature drawers. In the side lanes of this interesting district, you can observe Korean craftsmen at work in their street-side stalls.

Namdaemun Market Within walking distance of the Chosun Hotel, the Great South Gate Market is a colourful bazaar of open-air stalls selling local foodstuffs, contemporary clothing, bulk fabrics and miscellaneous household items. Always try to bargain for a better price in local markets; it is the accepted custom.

Tongdaemun Market Near the ancient Great East Gate on Chong Road, you'll find the biggest market in Korea. Spread over ten city blocks, the Great East Gate Market is divided into various buildings and byways, each specializing in different types of products. The main building, six storeys high and two blocks long, is where

the best bargains on Korean silk and synthetic brocades can be found. Row upon row of little stalls, their bolts of fabric spilling colourfully into the aisles, vie for the attention of passing shoppers.

Across the elevated highway from the main market hall is another massive building which specializes primarily in ready-made casual wear, shoes and sandals, and sundry household items. The shops in the vicinity of the nearby Seoul Stadium sell every conceivable variety of sports clothing and athletic equipment at bargain prices.

Itaewon Near the Yongsan Garrison, headquarters of America's Eighth Army Command, runs a broad boulevard known simply as Itaewon. It is a lively avenue of clothing shops, tailors, restaurants, coffee shops, bars and nightclubs, all of which are geared towards the tastes and budgets of American GI's stationed at Yongsan Garrison.

For export-quality, contemporary clothing, Itaewon is the best place in Seoul to shop. Stores here offer the latest styles in sports shirts, blouses, sweaters and other popular apparel at remarkably low prices. Jackets, belts, bags, wallets, shoes and other items of leather and eelskin are also good buys in Itaewon. There are also shops which specialize in brassware, lacquerware, antique reproductions and souvenirs. Almost all proprietors in Itaewon speak English well enough to conduct business with foreign customers.

Department Stores Seoul's major department stores are as big and modern as their counterparts in the West, and should be included on any serious shopper's itinerary. Located in and around the Myong-dong district, these huge emporia offer at fixed prices a full range of contemporary consumer products manufactured in Korea.

The biggest, most complete emporium in Seoul is the Lotte Shopping Centre, located adjacent to the Lotte Hotel. The eighth floor has a duty-free shop for tourists and is divided into a section for Korean products (ginseng, celadon, lacquerware, handicrafts and souvenirs) and a section for famous brand-name luxury items imported from abroad ('Gucci', 'Dunhill', 'Cardin' and 'Yves St Laurent'). The ninth and tenth floors have been converted into an interesting international 'Food Street', where two dozen restaurants offer various styles of Oriental and Occidental cuisine, from simple snacks to famous specialities.

Listed below are the names, addresses, phone numbers and official weekly holidays of Seoul's major department stores, which stay open from 10.30 am till 7.30 pm.

Lotte Shopping Centre	1 Sokong-dong Chung-ku	771–25	Tuesday

Midopa	123, 2-ka Namdaemun-ro Chung-ku	754−2222	Wednesday
Shinsegye	52−5, 1-ka Chungmu-ro Chung-ku	754−1234	Monday
Cheil	31−1, 2-ka Myong-dong Chung-ku	766−2741	Sunday
Hyundai	224−11 Apkujong-dong Kangnam-ku	547−2233	1st and 3rd Tuesdays

Shopping Arcades Seoul's shopping arcades are among the most extensive in Asia. Major downtown hotels such as the Chosun, Lotte and Seoul Plaza each have their own arcade of shops, which sell everything from celadon, silk and ginseng to cameras, watches, cosmetics and Western fashions.

Many of the underground passageways used by pedestrians to cross Seoul's traffic-jammed streets serve as vast shopping arcades too, especially in the downtown area. There are several street level arcades as well. Seoul's major shopping arcades are:

Underground: Bando Chosun (below the Chosun Hotel), Lotte First Avenue (below Lotte Hotel and Shopping Centre), Sokong (adjacent to Bando Chosun Arcade), Ulchi (beneath Ulchi Road, 2-ka), Chonggak (beneath Chong Road, 2-ka) and Haehyon (beneath Namdaemun Road, near Great East Gate).

Above ground: Pagoda (near Insadong and Pagoda Park), Seun (along Chong Road, 4-ka), Sampung (along Ulchi Road, 4-ka), Tongbang Building Arcade and Daewoo Building Arcade.

Duty-Free Shops Seoul provides foreign shoppers with a series of special duty-free shops and foreign commissaries for their exclusive use. The former sell famous Western luxury items, liquor and local handicrafts. You may use either local or foreign currencies, but you must present your passport upon purchase. Foreign commissaries stock common American foodstuffs, toiletries and other 'essential' items.

Duty-free shops are located at Kimpo Airport, the Lotte Shopping Centre (eighth floor), the Nam Moon Shop (5 Yang-dong, Chung-ku), Ungchon Co (15 Insadong, Chongro-ku) and the Tonghwa Shop (1−41 Sajik-dong, Chongro-ku). Foreign commissaries are located in the Chosun Hotel arcade, the Lotte basement arcade, Myong-dong and elsewhere about town.

Entertainment

Koreans play as enthusiastically by night as they work by day: the setting of the sun marks the end of the work day. Prodigious drinkers and generous hosts, Koreans are most sociable and relaxed at night, when Korea's sensual side blossoms, and one can enter the colourful 'Floating World' of nightlife.

Just as sunset signals the onset of evening entertainment in Seoul today, the stroke of midnight used to signal its abrupt demise. Until 1981, there was a strictly enforced midnight curfew. However, since the government lifted this long-standing curfew, the nervous tension has happily disappeared from nightlife in Seoul, and today the capital boasts a colourful and varied night scene.

Whether you seek Western- or Korean-style entertainment, modern or traditional ambiance, low-budget beer-halls or high-rolling nightclubs and casinos, Seoul has them all. For convenience, Western-style nightlife and Korean-style nightlife are described separately.

Western-Style Entertainment

In the West, a night on the town usually begins with a few 'happy hour' cocktails. In Seoul, the bars of the leading international hotels and European restaurants are the best places to savour genuine Western cocktails in an authentic Western atmosphere.

Seoul's most popular Western watering hole is the **Ninth Gate Bar**, located in the lobby of the Westin Chosun Hotel. Skilled bartenders, friendly waitresses and live music make this a popular place for Seoul's international community to settle unfinished business while celebrating the onset of evening.

Another spot with traditional Western atmosphere is the **Bobby London Pub** in the lower arcade of the Lotte Hotel. After a few drinks there you might think you're back in London. The bar at the **Banjul**, which has a good Western restaurant and a hostess club on its upper floors, is tastefully decorated and provides live music. Banjul is at 12–16 Gwanchul-dong, Chongro-ku, two lanes behind the Samilro Building.

Single men might like to start the evening by hoisting a few glasses at the **Tiger House**, diagonally across from the Chosun Hotel. At the Savoy Hotel's **Goody-Goody Bar** located in the basement, you're also likely to meet some of Seoul's swinging young sybarites.

After cocktails, dinner. Each of Seoul's leading deluxe hotels has at least one good gourmet restaurant featuring Western cuisine, and though prices tend to run rather high at these places, so do standards of food and service. Seoul's first gourmet French restaurant was the

Chosun's **Ninth Gate**, and it remains in high favour among the city's businessmen and gourmets. Recently renovated, the Ninth Gate strikes a pleasant balance between opulence and restraint, and the menu offers traditional favourites as well as innovative house specialities.

Of the 31 restaurants and bars operated by the Lotte Hotel, the **Prince Eugene** provides the most splendid luxury in dining. Its palatial decor is matched by one of the most beautiful menus in town — and some of the highest prices. The dessert menu is especially appealing. For a more subdued atmosphere, you might try the Hyatt Regency's **Hugo's Restaurant**, a fine Continental restaurant with a well established international reputation, or perhaps the **Celadon Restaurant** on the second floor of the Sheraton Walker Hill, where Korean celadon and German crystal complement a mouth-watering menu and superb service. Buffet fans will find Seoul's most bountiful buffet table, elaborately laden with Western as well as Japanese and Korean selections, at the Shilla Hotel's **Shangrila Restaurant**, which is built into a wing of the old Yi-Dynasty guest-house. For American beefsteaks cooked American style and served in an informal American atmosphere, try the **El Toro** on the second floor of the Seoul Plaza Hotel.

But if you wish to escape the hotels and their high prices, there are also a few places on the outside which serve good Western food in pleasant surroundings. **La Cantina** (tel. 771−2579), located directly across from the Lotte Hotel in the basement of the Sam Sun Building, serves authentic Italian cuisine at reasonable prices and is quite popular with Seoul's resident foreign community. At **Banjul**, mentioned above, an extensive menu with both Eastern and Western flavours awaits the discriminating diner, and excellent music enhances the pleasure of dining there. Or you could rub shoulders with some of Korea's most popular entertainers, many of whom dine Western-style at the **Hee Joon**, a cosy dinner club with live music located in the basement of the Kuk-dong Building.

Once fortified with drinks and dinner, you can consider further evening entertainment. Seoul has a number of interesting theatre-restaurants, which feature excellent entertainment but only mediocre meals. Gourmets are advised to take their meals elsewhere, then arrive in time for the show, which usually begins around 8.30 pm. The **Kayagum Theatre Restaurant** at the Sheraton Walker Hill stages the most extravagant and colourful floorshows in town, with acts and atmosphere reminiscent of Las Vegas. For more local flavour, the **World Cup Theatre Restaurant** stages a dazzling variety show with stars from Korea's show-biz world, as well as occasional foreign talents. Two other popular theatre-restaurants in Seoul are the Pacific Hotel's **Holiday Inn** and the **Tiffany**, located in the basement of the Tongmin Building, behind City Hall.

If gambling is your game, then catch a cab up to the Sheraton Walker Hill, where a spacious casino provides the inveterate bettor with ample opportunity to try his luck at various games of chance. There are currently 11 licensed casinos operating in Korea, each at a different tourist centre.

Connoisseurs of classical music should try to attend a concert, opera or symphony while in Seoul. Unlike some other Asians, Koreans have a truly fine ear and genuine talent for classical Western music. The new **Sejong Cultural Centre,** located opposite the American Embassy on Sejong Road, and the **National Theatre** — home of Korea's renowned National Ballet, National Symphony, and National Opera — both stage regular performances featuring famous Korean as well as international musicians, singers and dancers.

On the other hand, if the throbbing rhythms of pop-music and disco-dancing appeal to you more, the boogie scene in Seoul by night should suffice. At **Ob's Cabin**, a four-floor music club popular with Seoul's foreign community, pop singers and rock bands belt out the latest tunes on stage. Ob's is in the heart of the ever-popular Myong-dong district, two lanes behind Unesco House. **All That Jazz**, located at 168–17 Itaewon-dong, is Seoul's best jazz club, featuring American disc-jockeys, American atmosphere and live jam sessions three times a week.

Most of Seoul's leading international hotels feature lively disco-clubs. The Lotte's **Annabelle's**, the Chosun's **Club Tomorrow** and the Shilla's **Club Universe** are very popular, as are the discos at the Hyatt and Sheraton Walker Hill. Another good dancing club is the new **Club Copacabana**, located in a narrow lane behind Tiffany's, where American DJ's spin discs for two floors of dancers. Seoul's disco-clubs are equally enjoyable for couples and for singles, and unattached guests usually have no problem finding willing partners.

Those who prefer funky atmosphere and low prices to the expensive glitter of deluxe hotel discos should venture over to the honky-tonk clubs and bars of Itaewon. The most popular (and safest) disco-club in Itaewon is the swinging **Sportsman's Club**, located on the third floor of a building near the New Yongsan Hotel. The Sportsman's has the least expensive Western liquor in town, no cover charge, American management, and a colourful menagerie of Seoul's young swingers — mostly Western men and Korean women. A team of brawny bouncers keeps the peace at the Sportsman's, effectively preventing the fist-fights which occasionally erupt in Itaewon's less reputable establishments. Just down the street is the similar but less crowded **Servicemen's Club**. Both of these places blossom after 9 pm, and usually stay open for as long as you can stay on your feet. If discos are simply not your style, a good way to wind up the evening is with a few nightcaps at The Chosun's Ninth Gate Bar or the Lotte's Bobby London Pub, where you are more than likely to meet a few fellow night-owls as well as some other interesting people.

Korean-Style Entertainment

Like Westerners, Koreans like to greet the evening with a few drinks among friends. However, in Korea liquor of any sort is always taken together with *anju* (drinking snacks), which can range from a handful of peanuts and a few leaves of dried seaweed to a sumptuous array of dozens of hot and cold dishes sufficient to make a meal in itself.

Myong-dong and other districts in downtown Seoul are full of typical Korean taverns and restaurants, and most of them can be identified easily by sight. Starting with the simplest, you could try a small bottle of sweet potato wine at a local *soju*-house — small, noisy, smoke-filled taverns where ruddy-faced workers toast each other boisterously while snacking on excellent *anju* — but take it easy with *soju* because in excess it tends to leave a nasty hangover. Behind the theatre at Kwanghwamun, under the first 'Jinro Limited' sign, is **Chongil Chip**, one of Seoul's more interesting *soju*-houses. Even simpler than these are the *pojang-macha*, tent wagons with red-white-and-blue awnings located in alleys and byways all over Seoul. One of the best usually appears at night up the alley next to the Samilro Building.

A step up from *soju* on the drinking scale is *makkolli*, a refined rice wine which is Korea's most popular drink. **Tae Ryon** and **Chonggey-Oke**, both located across the street east of the Samilro Building, are typical *makkolli*-houses which serve particularly tasty *anju*. Behind the new high-rise at the Kwanghwamun intersection, each with a blue 'Jinro Limited' sign over the door, stand four *makkolli*-houses in a row, where you can drink *yakchu* (highly refined *makkolli*) and sample the excellent *pindaetok* (shrimp-studded pancakes of mung-bean) and *chogaetang* (clam soup).

For foreigners, the most popular type of Korean drinking establishment seems to be the beer-hall, where chilled beer and simple snacks are served. Small and cosy, beer-halls can become quite lively. They are easily identified by square red signs with a frothy mug of beer floating inside a white ring, often with the little 'OB Beer' logo. There are numerous beer-halls located within a single lane two

blocks behind the Seoul Plaza Hotel in the direction of South Gate,
including the **Blue Villa**. Or simply stroll through Myong-dong until
you see a place that strikes your fancy. Beer halls are convenient,
inexpensive places to stop for a rest and a refreshing cold brew —
especially welcome during the summer.

A more contemporary style of Korean bistro is the stand-bar.
These are tastefully decorated taverns where customers sit at long bars
while hostesses serve them beer or whisky and *anju* and sometimes sit
and chat for a while. Stand-bars are most popular among businessmen
and office workers, who flock there after work to unwind.

By the time you leave a typical Korean *sul-jip* (liquor house), you
should be ready for a hearty meal at a typical Korean *sik-tang*
(restaurant). Korean restaurants range from little hole-in-the-wall
eateries specializing in a single type of dish to elaborate multi-stored
food palaces with a wide variety of selections. If you choose the
former, which certainly provide the most authentic Korean
atmosphere, remember that English is generally not understood, so
simply point out whatever looks good in the window or on other
tables.

Barbecued beef is the hallmark of gourmet Korean cuisine. Good
Korean beef-houses are easily identified by the round hole in the
centre of each table, which accommodates the brazier. Try the **Buil
Barbecued Rib House**, located on Ulchi Road, or the famous **Han Il
Kwan**, a well established chain of gourmet Korean restaurants with
excellent branches in Myong-dong and Chong-ro. Simply walk in and
say '*bulgogi*' or '*kalbi*' and everything will be taken care of.

Another related form of Korean beef cookery uses a heavy iron
griddle upon which diced beefsteak and fresh Oriental vegetables are
sautéed in front of you. Seoul's most popular roast beef restaurant is
the **Pine Hill**, a modern, multi-storied establishment located downtown
at 88−5, 2-ka, Ju-dong, Chung-ku. Another delightful 'iron-plate' beef
restaurant is located in the heart of Insadong, Seoul's antique and art
gallery district. It is called the **Gourmet**, and here you may enjoy your
grilled beef and vegetables in private booths.

Besides offering beef, Korean restaurants also specialize in
seafood, noodles and chicken. The **Hamkung Naengmyon**, located in
Myong-dong across from the Unesco House, is one of Seoul's most
famous buckwheat-noodle houses, and here you will be welcomed to
the premises by a talking bird. Korean chicken is a truly unique native
treat. Try it at the **Paekche Ginseng Chicken Restaurant**, located in a
narrow passageway just behind the Commercial Bank of Korea off
Myong-dong's main drag. Look for the sign with the Chinese
characters and an arrow pointing down the passageway. Accompanied

by a few shots of Jinro Ginseng wine and topped off with a glass of fresh-squeezed ginseng juice, this meal provides a wonderful blend of food and medicine.

Of course, you may wish to sample the full range of gourmet Korean cuisine at the fancy, and rather expensive, Korean restaurants in some of Seoul's major hotels. The Shilla's **Sorabol** and the Lotte's **Mugunghwa** serve traditional Korean fare in an elegant ambiance, and English menus are available. For even more variety in dining, you could visit the ninth and tenth floors of the Lotte Shopping Centre, which have been converted into a special culinary arcade for tourists called **Food Street**. Here, two dozen cosy little restaurants specialize in a wide range of Korean, Japanese and Chinese cuisine. Or you could opt for an evening at **Korea House**, where you may reserve a private dining area in the traditional *ondol* (warm-floor) rooms. For those who prefer tables and chairs, Korea House also offers a sumptuous buffet of Korean cuisine served in a Western-style dining room. After dinner, you can watch a programme of traditional Korean entertainment, including folk dances, mask-dance drama, classical Korean music, acrobatics and other performances.

For a more contemporary but only slightly less expensive version of the traditional Korean *kisaeng* house, try a Korean salon. Salon service is essentially the same as *kisaeng*, except that the setting is decidedly modern: tables and chairs replace the cushions and *ondol*-floors, and hostesses dress in contemporary fashions rather than in traditional *hanbok*. Salons abound throughout Seoul, and are often identified by the word 'salon' in English on a sign over the door — a reflection of their modern orientation.

Among Koreans, the most popular form of after-dinner entertainment is good music and conversation over a few drinks with friends. Indeed, drinking establishments with music are one of the most salient features of contemporary Korean leisure life, for they combine two of Korea's favourite pastimes. At the **Sansoo Gapsam**, located about 90 metres (100 yards) behind Tiffany, is Seoul's best classical music beer-hall, where string quartets and soloists serenade customers seated at cosy tables. For the same experience with rock music, visit **Ob's Cabin**, referred to above in the Western section.

Musical coffee shops and *tabang* (tearooms) can usually be identified by the English word 'music', or a few musical notes dancing next to a picture of a coffee cup on a sign by the entrance. Usually located in the basement or second floor of office buildings, they are as common in Seoul as cafés are in Paris. A good example is the **Yack Sock**, located on the second floor directly across the street from the World Cup Theatre Restaurant. Here folk singers and records entertain a chatting clientele ensconced in dimly lit booths. Other popular *tabang* include the **Maronie**, located next to Citibank near the Chosun Hotel, and the **Chungja**, located in the basement of Ms Shopping Centre in Myong-dong. Both are frequented by young people with a taste for pop music. For a quieter atmosphere and more classical music, try the **June**, or the **Phil Harmony**, both located directly across the street from the Savoy Hotel. Equally appropriate for discreet rendezvous or casual business discussions, *tabang* are great places to relax and observe Koreans at leisure. You might even make some new friends there.

Couples who seek a somewhat more romantic atmosphere may sip drinks in the comfort of a contemporary Korean lounge, such as the **Café Temptation**, identified by an odd top hat logo just off the street about 200 metres (220 yards) west of the Samilro Building. A similar lounge with tasteful, contemporary decor and intimate ambiance is the **Han Madang**, opposite the old guard tower east of the capital building. Just in front of Ob's Cabin in Myong-dong is a cosy four-floor complex, fostering a romantic mood, called **Duju Bal**. All of these places cater to amorous couples, with quiet nooks where they can escape the crowded streets of Seoul.

Excursions from Seoul

Within easy access of Seoul are many interesting historical sites, ancient temples, old fortresses, mountain parks, royal tombs and cultural relics. The traveller without sufficient time to tour the scenic southern and coastal provinces of Korea should at least try to make a few of these side trips during his stay in Seoul. Otherwise he will miss the true flavour and feeling of Korea. Seoul itself, like any other modern metropolis, is a jumble of concrete and steel. Though there are places in town where you may still catch glimpses of old Korea, you must leave the city limits in order to get a complete picture of Korea and her heritage. Each of the destinations described below may be covered from Seoul in a single day, although several of them merit an overnight stay should time permit.

Transportation in and out of the capital is modern and efficient, with regular bus and train service in all directions, and convenient organized tours cover most of the destinations. However, if your budget permits, the best way to visit any place in Korea outside of Seoul is by private car. Either retain a taxi for a whole day, or rent a car and drive yourself. Korea's excellent expressway system is a pleasure to drive, and the high cost of private cars in Korea keeps highway traffic to an absolute minimum.

Ginseng: The Mysterious Man-root

Ginseng (*insam* in Korean) is the mysterious 'man-root' of the East and one of Korea's most valuable assets. In fact, ginseng has almost become a universally recognized symbol of Korea. Due to the root's uncanny resemblance to the human form, the Chinese characters which denote ginseng include the ideogram for 'man'.

Ginseng has been used for almost 5,000 years in China and Korea, and it first appeared in written prescriptions in ancient Chinese medical manuals over 2,000 years ago. Korea has been a major supplier of ginseng to China and Japan for at least 1,500 years. When Korea established a tributary relationship with China 500 years ago, the main item demanded by the Chinese court as annual tribute was ginseng.

Though it has been used as a remedy in the East for five millennia, only recently has the efficacy of this amazing herb been proven to the satisfaction of sceptical Western science. Soviet scientists recently isolated three active components in ginseng — panaxin, panquilan and schingenin — which in combination have been shown to significantly enhance circulation, stimulate the nervous system and increase secretions of vital hormones. These are precisely the therapeutic effects attributed to ginseng by traditional Chinese medicine.

Even more significant, the Soviet scientists claim that ginseng emits minute amounts of a unique band of ultraviolet radiation that specifically stimulates the rapid growth of healthy human tissue. This healing energy has been known to Chinese and Korean physicians for many millennia. The combination of potent biochemicals and active bioenergy is what makes ginseng such a powerful therapeutic herb.

However, it is not only ailing patients who use ginseng. Soviet and Eastern European athletes have been using it for years to enhance their stamina and improve their performance in athletic competition, and perhaps this at least partly accounts for their rich harvests of gold and

Ginseng comes in red and white varieties, and is carefully sorted for quality and age.

silver medals at Olympic and other international sporting events. Korean athletes use it as well, and in the 1986 Asia Games they displaced Japan as the runner-up to China in the final medal count.

Originally found in remote wild mountains in northern Korea and Manchuria, ginseng is now cultivated on a large scale throughout the Korean peninsula. You will see it growing everywhere, especially on Kanghwa Island, in long, neat rows protected from sun, wind and rain by thatched shelters. Cultivated ginseng roots require constant care and grow to maturity in four to six years. After harvesting, the roots are washed, peeled, steamed and dried, then sorted according to age and quality. Ginseng depletes soil so completely that nothing will grow there again for at least ten years. This absorption of nutrients from the earth is the source of the root's medicinal potency. Exports of ginseng and related products earn Korea almost US$200 million annually, which makes the 'man root' vital to Korea's economy as well as its traditional medical arts.

There are two types of ginseng: white (*baek*) and red (*hong*). The white variety is more common and less expensive and is usually recommended for summer use. The red type is considerably more potent and about four times as expensive and is most appropriate for winter use. Most red ginseng is exported, which makes it relatively difficult to find in Korea.

The variety of products made in Korea from ginseng is incredible. In addition to the gangly root itself, you can buy ginseng pills, powder, liquid extract, candy, chewing gum, jam, tea, wine, skin cream, soap, shampoo — even ginseng cigarettes! Remember, however, that the key to ginseng therapy is not large concentrated doses, but rather small, regular doses taken over a prolonged period of time. The one affliction for which a strong single dose of ginseng seems to work wonders is an alcohol hangover.

The way ginseng actually works is a subject of great interest to medical scientists today, especially in Japan and Korea. Most researchers agree it stimulates the body's own natural functions, especially metabolism, circulation and immunity. According to Dr Kuniyoshi Kisaki of Japan, 'Ginseng itself is not a nutrient, but it seems to stimulate the metabolism of the body, resulting in increased activity of synthesizing fresh cells'. It has also been shown to have a powerful anti-oxidant activity, much like Vitamin E, which makes it a highly beneficial anti-ageing supplement. Clinical tests in Japan have shown that ginseng significantly increases the chance of survival and hastens the recovery of patients undergoing radiation and chemotherapy for cancer. It does this by helping the body detoxify and by tonifying liver function, which is severely impaired by conventional cancer therapy. Dr Ma Chun of Shanghai goes even further, declaring, 'All cancer patients should take ginseng every day, regardless of what other therapy they use, because ginseng greatly enhances the body's natural ability to heal itself'.

Despite the proliferation of modern ginseng products, the traditional infusion of the dried root remains the most effective and pleasant way to take it. *Insam cha jip* (ginseng tea rooms) are located in every city and town in Korea and are readily identified by a large humanoid ginseng root painted on the door. Instead of a coffee break, take a ginseng break whenever travelling in Korea and note what a pleasant lift it gives.

One of the best therapeutic ginseng brews is prepared by boiling sliced white ginseng, dried red jujubes (Chinese dates) and pine seeds with a little raw sugar or honey in water. Taken as a tonic throughout the day, this potion increases strength (especially in the legs), enhances circulation, stimulates metabolism and retards aging. Hung Wu-fan, father of Taiwan's most renowned martial artist Hung Yi-hsiang, drank this brew every day of his adult life and lived to the ripe old age of 96.

Inevitably, any drug that proves effective in promoting longevity and preventing disease ends up being touted as an aphrodisiac as well, and ginseng is no exception. In fact, ginseng does improve sexual performance as a 'side effect' of its powerful stimulatory effects on the entire endocrine system. The resulting enhancement of hormone secretions naturally enhances sexual potency. Studies in Japan have also shown that ginseng is highly effective in curing sexual frigidity in women.

Korean ginseng production and distribution are strictly controlled by a government monopoly bureau. This bureau rigorously controls quality and sets prices for the various grades of ginseng. Ordinary grades sell anywhere from US$0.35 to $8 per gram (US$10 to $225 per ounce), but in Hong Kong you can find *la crème de la crème* from Manchuria — long spindly wild roots, often over 100 years old — that sells for up to US$700 per gram (US$20,000 per ounce)! Asked who buys this precious product, a Chinese clerk replied, 'Very old, very wealthy men who are on their deathbeds and wish to live a few more days'.

Ginseng is sold throughout Korea, and since the prices are fixed, it costs the same everywhere. Regardless of price, which always reflects quality, ginseng remains one of the very best bargains in Korea, for it is a long-term investment in health and longevity that pays dividends day by day.

Recipe for Longevity Tea

In a ceramic or pyrex glass (not metal) pot, pour one litre (3.5 cups) of water and bring to a boil with the following ingredients:

6 thin slices of white ginseng
6 red jujubes (crushed with pliers until the kernel inside cracks)
¼ cup raw pine seeds
1–2 teaspoons raw sugar or honey

Cover and simmer slowly for 20 minutes. Pour into tea cups and drink warm. When brew is almost finished add another one half litre water and boil for another 15 minutes.

Kanghwa-do: Isle of Exile

About 50 kilometres (30 miles) northwest of Seoul lies historic
Kanghwa Island, with cultural relics spanning Korea's entire history.
Buses leave regularly for Kanghwa-do (*do* means island) from Seoul's
Sinchon Rotary, and the trip takes about 1.5 hours.

As you cross Yomha Strait to enter the island, note the remains of
walls and fortresses constructed during the mid-13th century. These
were built to protect the royal family, who took refuge here during the
Mongol invasions. Kanghwa City lies just behind these fortifications.

The town itself is small and rustic, a perfect place for leisurely
strolls and for absorbing local colour. Here one finds some of Korea's
finest floor mats, doorway screens, and baskets woven of rush. The
town is also an important silk weaving centre.

Next to the silk factory, hanging in a small pavilion, is a 3,864-
kilogram (8,500-pound) bronze bell cast during the reign of King
Sukchong (reigned 1674–1720). When French troops stormed the
island in 1866 in a raid to avenge the execution of nine French Catholic
priests in Seoul, they tried to carry away this bell as booty, but they
found it too heavy and abandoned it before reaching their ships.

Further up the road is the restored palace of King Kojong, who
lived there in exile for 39 years as the Koryo Dynasty tried
unsuccessfully to resist the Mongol invasions. Lower down the hill,
along a narrow pathway, is one of Kanghwa's most interesting
structures: Korea's oldest Episcopal Church, built in 1900 by Bishop
Charles Korfe. An old Bodhi tree, of the type under which Buddha is
said to have gained enlightenment, was planted there at the church's
dedication and still stands in the southwest corner of the compound.
This church harmoniously blends Chinese, Christian and Korean styles
in architectural design, and the symbols which embellish it reflect
Taoist, Buddhist and Christian elements.

En route back to town, you might want to stop to visit the exotic
sacred altar constructed of three enormous flat boulders and erected
during palaeolithic times.

On the southern part of the island stands Mt Mani, with Tangun's
Altar at the summit. Though the actual origins of this altar remain
unknown, legend has it that Tangun himself established it for worship
when he founded Korea in 2333 BC. The 500-metre (1650-foot) climb
to the top may take your breath away, but so will the marvellous
panoramic views from the summit.

Sixteen kilometres (10 miles) south of town and two kilometres (1.2
miles) east of Mt Mani stands Chongdung-sa, one of Korea's oldest
temples. Built in AD 381, it is the site where the 80,000 wood-blocks

of the Tripitaka Koreana were carved; a mammoth task which took 19 years to complete. Of particular interest are four figures, squatting uncomfortably with their chins pressed to their knees, which hold up the eaves of the main hall. According to the story, the builder assigned to renovate the temple after the Japanese depradations of 1592−8 fell in love with the beautiful young daughter of a local tavern owner there. She agreed to marry him when his work at the temple was complete, but on the appointed day the hapless old builder found that his fiancée had eloped with a younger man. As revenge, he carved four figures of her, naked and crouching in eternal pain, to hold up the roof of the main hall.

For those with a taste for temples, there is one more excursion worth taking on Kanghwa Island, to Pomun-sa, a 1,400-year-old temple which has been beautifully restored. To get there, head to Kanghwa's west coast, then ferry across to nearby Songmo Island. Next comes a jolting 45-minute bus ride. The site commands a fine view of the Yellow Sea and the dozens of odd-shaped islands which dot it. In a stone chamber behind the temple sit 22 stone Buddhas, each enshrined in an individual wall niche. One last strenuous hike takes you up to the famous Eyebrow Rock Buddha, concavely carved into a sheer granite cliff overlooking the Yellow Sea.

Panmunjom: Window onto the North

Only 56 kilometres (35 miles) north of Seoul is the Demilitarized Zone (DMZ), which separates North from South Korea. Straddling the DMZ is the village of Panmunjom, where over 400 official meetings between North and South have been held since the Korean Armistice was signed on 27 July 1953.

'Demilitarized Zone' seems a rather inappropriate name for this five-kilometre (three-mile) wide belt of no man's land, which is heavily mined, constantly patrolled and bristling with barbed-wire, with one million troops armed to the teeth facing each other across it.

The United Nations Command (UNC) has authorized the Korean Tourism Bureau (KTB) to run regular tours up to Panmunjom for foreign tourists. KTB has offices in the Koreana and Lotte Hotels, and agents in most other deluxe hotels, where bookings for this tour must be made at least 48 hours in advance. You must bring your passport, and not wear faded blue jeans or sloppy clothes of any kind. According to the guide, North Korean infiltrators often cross the DMZ disguised as rustic farmers, who generally wear old, faded clothing.

En route to Panmunjom, the bus stops at several Korean War memorials, erected in honour of the 16 nations who sent troops to fight alongside South Koreans under United Nations command. To reach the UN command post along the DMZ, one crosses the Bridge of Freedom over the Imjun River. Veterans of the war say that so many people were killed and wounded in the battles, which raged across the Imjun, that the river ran red with blood.

On reaching the command post, you will receive an official briefing from an American military officer and a typical American lunch at the cafeteria. Then the bus takes you into the Joint Security Area, where the truce talks are actually held. Here you will see the Conference Room, neatly and evenly divided between North and South, and Freedom House, an elevated Korean pavilion from which you may gaze across to the world's most secluded land.

A hundred metres (110 yards) below the Conference Room is the Bridge of No Return, so named because at the end of the war all prisoners were given a final choice between North and South here. On the southern side of the bridge stands the charred remains of a tree. Routine trimming of this tree by UN guards triggered the infamous incident in which Northern troops stormed across the Bridge of No Return swinging axes and clubs, killing two American soldiers and wounding four. To prevent such attacks in the future, a large truck and driver are now permanently stationed on the Southern side, with motor running, clutch depressed and gear set in reverse at all times. Should Northern guards attempt to rush across the bridge again, the driver will block the bridge long enough to evacuate or reinforce UNC personnel.

Today, 1,000 American troops are kept permanently stationed among the joint UNC forces protecting the DMZ. They serve voluntarily for one year at a time, and they must meet three stringent conditions: they must stand at least 1.8 metres (six feet) tall, weigh over 77 kilograms (170 pounds), and score highly on a rigorous aptitude test.

Suwon City and the Korean Folk Village

Suwon, which means 'source of water' due to the fine artesian wells there, is both a contemporary provincial capital and an ancient fortress city. Situated only 51 kilometres (31 miles) south of Seoul, Suwon's culinary claim to fame are the luscious red strawberries produced there in spring and summer. To get there, take the regular electric subway train from Seoul's City Hall station, or take the bus from the Kolon Express Terminal in Cho-dong.

The entire town is encircled by a massive 5.5-kilometre (3.4-mile) fortress wall, segments of which are connected by ancient city gates dating back to the Yi Dynasty. Here King Chongjo, who actually contemplated moving the kingdom's capital from Seoul to Suwon, built the famous Flower Fortress, complete with parapets, pavilions, elevated platforms, domes, gates and parade grounds. In 1975, the Korean government embarked on a W3.3-billion project to restore this classical fortress to its original splendour.

Stroll up to the city's North Gate (*Changam-mun*), where an exquisitely landscaped pond is set just below a lovely moon-gazing pavilion. Here King Chongjo used to relax with his ladies and watch the reflection of the moon crossing the mirror surface of the pond.

Near Suwon City is the Korean Folk Village, a complex of 240 homes, shops, taverns and other authentic Yi-Dynasty structures, built entirely with private funds and open to the public daily from 10 am to 5 pm. The village is located about 20 minutes by cab from Suwon, and the ride costs about W4,000. If you prefer to go directly from Seoul without stopping in Suwon, most of Seoul's tourist agencies run packaged, one-day tours to the Korean Folk Village.

In this charming village, it is easy to imagine you are in ancient Korea. With their traditional garments, ancient implements and 'movie-set' dwellings, the people actually live and work; the entire Korean Folk Village is a functioning community. Here you will see a young woman clad in *hanbok* pounding rice into flour in an old stone mortar; you will find blacksmiths forging traditional tools, and a bride and groom performing the time-honoured Confucian wedding rituals.

Inchon

Lying 39 kilometres (24 miles) due west of Seoul, Inchon is Korea's fourth largest city and third most important port. The traditional port-of-entry for foreigners, who prior to 1882 were prohibited from visiting points further inland, Inchon was twice attacked by American ships and once by the French. It was officially opened to foreign trade and diplomatic missions by the signing of the Korean-American Treaty of Amity and Commerce in 1882.

Inchon was the site of General Douglas MacArthur's daring pre-dawn amphibious landing on 15 September 1950, a coup which turned the tide of the Korean War. After 12 days of bloody fighting, this landing led to the recapture of Seoul from communist forces. Atop **Freedom Hill**, facing the Yellow Sea, stands a ten-metre (33-foot) statue of General MacArthur, who remains a much respected hero in Korea.

Today Inchon is a busy shipping and industrial town with relatively few historical sites of interest to the tourist. Nearby are the beaches of Song-do, which remain perpetually crowded during the summer, but if you have enough time you can take a ferry across to some of the more remote outer islands, or down the west coast, where there are cleaner, less crowded beaches and lovely lagoons.

Perhaps Inchon's greatest attraction is the excellent seafood served in rustic restaurants on some of the nearby islands such as **Wolmi** and **Sowolmi**. Gourmet creations of raw fish are their specialities.

Inchon boasts a deluxe hotel called the **Olympus**, with 200 rooms, a nightclub, a casino, a large swimming pool, and both Korean and Western restaurants. Local inns offer less expensive and more traditional accommodation. The expressway takes you to Inchon from Seoul in less than 30 minutes.

The North and South Han Mountain Fortresses

Pukansansong and **Namhansansong** are two major fortresses in the vicinity of Seoul. These ancient battlements date back to the early Paekche period 2,000 years ago, after which they fell into disuse until the 17th century, when the kings of Yi refortified them in the face of Manchu invasions.

The northern fortress is located to the northeast of Seoul and skirts the ridges of Pukan (Northern Han) Mountain. With this historic site as a background, the surrounding forests, meadows and streams are popular places for hiking and picnics. The mountain slopes abound with ancient temples, fortress ruins and other archaeological relics.

Thirty kilometres (19 miles) southeast of Seoul, the walls and 17 gates of the southern fortress snake eight kilometres (five miles) along Namhan (Southern Han) Mountain. This impressive fortification, which stands over six metres (20 feet) high in places, is the more popular of the two. It was here in 1636 that King Injo finally surrendered to invading Manchu forces. On a clear day, the summit affords spectacular views of the Han River valley.

Royal Tombs

Royal burial grounds rank among Korea's most tranquil and scenic settings, and there are numerous such parks in the Seoul area. Korean tombs, unlike the gaudy burial palaces of Chinese emperors, blend simply and quietly into their natural surroundings. The underground chambers are covered over with round mounds of earth and domed with layers of green turf. They are marked with simple but elegant stone shrines and set serenely among groves of pine and bamboo, the

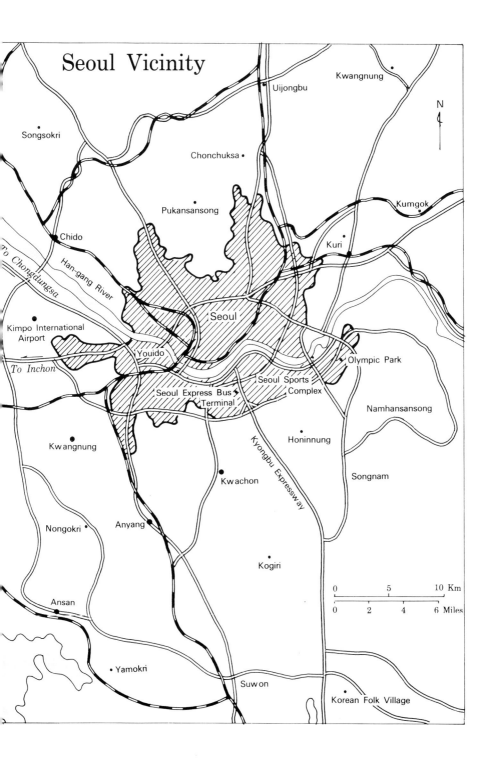

traditional Korean symbols of longevity. At first glance, the tombs appear to be natural, geometrical hills swelling up from the earth.

At Kumgok, about 40 minutes northeast of Seoul by car, lie the **Hong Yurung Tombs**, gravesites of Korea's last two kings (Kokjong and Sonjong) and their wives. Set in a wooded park full of magpies, orioles and cuckoos, these classical Korean burial mounds are perfect examples of the tranquil, naturally landscaped, earth-bound settings preferred by Korean kings for their final resting places. White stone guardians — including warriors, scholars and a host of mythical animals from the Oriental zodiac — line the approach to these tombs, much like the giant stone statues which keep eternal vigil over the route to the Ming imperial tombs north of Beijing.

Near Kumgok is **Tonggu-rung**, where King Taejo, founder of the Yi Dynasty, was buried in 1408. A little further north at **Kwangnung**, 28 kilometres (17 miles) out of Seoul, lies the most idyllic royal burial park in the Seoul area — the burial grounds of King Sejo (died 1468) and his wife Queen Yum Chon-hi. These magnificent mounds lie deep in thick forests of ancient trees. The meadows and streams of this wooded hideaway make excellent picnic grounds. Within the Kwangnung forest you will also find **Pongson Temple**, recently renovated in traditional style.

Just beyond the southeastern suburbs of Seoul are **Honnung**, the tombs of King Taejong (reigned 1367–1422) and Queen Wonkyong. At **Innung**, are the tombs of King Sunjo (reigned 1790–1834) and Queen Sunwon. These burial parks are located in fertile farmlands renowned for fresh melons and juicy strawberries. You may enjoy these succulent fruits in little *alfresco* fruit-stalls throughout the spring and summer seasons. The tombs are all protected by rows of stone guardians similar to those at Hong Yurung, and the surrounding park grounds are exceptionally well manicured.

Mount Sogni National Park

Sogni means 'Escape from the Vulgar'. A visit to this lovely mountain retreat, located in the very heart of Korea's central highlands, will certainly lift your spirits and soothe your senses. You can get there by taking a train from Seoul to Taechon, then transfering to a local bus or cab for the ride up to Mt Sogni. Alternatively, drive south from Seoul along the Seoul-Pusan Expressway, then turn off at the Chongju exit and follow the signs to Mt Sogni from there. The one-way drive by car takes about three hours, but is worth every minute.

After leaving the expressway and passing through the town of Chongju, you enter the winding **Malti Pass**, which leads up to Mt

Sogni's summit. Charming views of Korean rural life unfold on both sides of the road as you enter rolling forested foothills and pass through verdant valleys of neatly tended fields and paddies. Ancient ancestral shrines crop up with increasing frequency as you approach the summit. Towards the final route to the top stands the Chong-I'pum Pine, a stately old pine tree which is said to have raised its boughs in respect one day as King Sejo and his entourage passed by. Flattered and impressed by the tree's reverent gesture, the king conferred upon it the rank of *Chong-i'pum*, a title equivalent to that of a cabinet minister.

En route you will also pass a beautiful little village to the left of the road which, despite its ancient ambiance and classical style, is brand new. Each dwelling has the curving tiled roof, the corniced walls, the ornate covered portico and the graceful lines of a Silla-era country house, plus the conveniences of electricity, running water and modern appliances. This is typical of the new settlements sponsored by the New Community (Saemaul) Movement, a government campaign to raise the living standards of Korea's rural populace without sacrificing the flavour of their ancient traditions.

The mountain village of **Sogni-dong** serves as a launching point for hikes up to the 22 temples and pavilions scattered among Mt Sogni's craggy peaks and wooded valleys. This village is famous for its meals of wild mountain mushrooms, which are gathered in the area and sold at numerous roadside stalls. A large tourist hotel provides comfortable accommodation and a variety of recreational facilities for dedicated alpinists who wish to stay there for a night or two in order to explore this bucolic mountain park thoroughly. There are also a number of small Korean inns (*yogwan*). Sogni is beautiful in all four seasons, but especially in the autumn, when the forests of maple, oak and gingko trees radiate shades of red and gold.

Sogni's greatest attraction is **Popju-sa**, an ancient Buddhist temple founded in AD 553 by the great priest Uishin of Silla. Once this ranked among Korea's greatest temples; over 3,000 monks lived there on generous royal subsidies from devout Korean kings. Numerous ancient relics are preserved here, including an enormous iron rice-pot 1.2 metres (four feet) high and 2.7 metres (8.9 feet) in diameter, which was cast in AD 720 and used for cooking the monks' rice. There are also several ancient stone lanterns, an eighth-century stone tub shaped like a lotus, and an unusual five-storey image hall which dominates the central courtyard. Not so ancient but equally impressive is the 26-metre (86-foot) concrete Miruk Buddha of the Future, completed in 1964 and described as the biggest Buddha in Korea. If time and energy permit, trek along some of Sogni's excellent hiking trails up to the ridges above the Popju Temple for exquisite sweeping views of the temple complex and surrounding scenery.

Sanjong Lake

Northeast of Seoul lies picturesque Sanjong Lake, an artificial lake resort built by the Japanese during their occupation of Korea. North Korea's dictator Kim Il-sung kept a summer villa here prior to the Korean War, when the area lay within northern jurisdiction. Today Sanjong Lake is very popular among Seoul's inhabitants for hiking and picnics in the summer, and for skating in the winter.

En route to or from Sanjong Lake, you might consider a stop at the **Kyongguk Temple**, perhaps the most beautifully landscaped temple complex near Seoul. The serenity and natural beauty of this temple and its grounds offer refreshing respite from the hustle and bustle of the city.

There are many other scenic and historical sights within the vicinity of Seoul, but those described above are the most interesting and accessible. Those who have the time and the inclination to travel further afield should visit Korea's southern and coastal provinces, where the true flavour of Korea remains fresh and unspoiled, and where distractions from the modern world are minimal. Start your trip in and around Seoul, and if you find that you have a genuine taste for Korea, then plan to leave the crowded capital and proceed along the 'tourist trail' mapped out in the following chapters.

Han River Lake Resorts

Korea's most scenic lake country is about 1.5-hour's drive northeast of Seoul. The northeast province of Kangwon-do is a land of misty mountains, shimmering lakes, meandering rivers and fertile valleys neatly sculpted into green rice paddies and vegetable patches. The lakes created by the Soyang and Paltang dams are dotted with pleasant resorts which have become favourite holiday destinations for Seoul's inhabitants. Either rent a car and drive northeast along Highway 46 towards **Chunchon**, or catch a bus from Seoul's Chongnyang-ni Station.

A good place to spend a night or two before reaching Chunchon is **Nami-Som Island**, set in the middle of the Han River, about an hour's drive out of Seoul. There are regular ferries to the island, where you can rent a cosy bungalow and relax in utter tranquility among whispering pines, singing birds and placid waters.

Lakes and Sights

Twenty kilometres (12 miles) further north lies Chunchon and, if you're not driving, the most scenic route is by riverboat. **Chunchon Lake** and other nearby waterways form Korea's most exquisite lake resort country and have fishing, sailing, swimming, water-skiing and

Three dancers from one of the many provincial dance troupes.

other recreational activities. **Ethiopia House**, a Korean teahouse set above the shores of the lake, is a good place to refresh yourself and take in the expansive views. Ferryboats run regularly to various scenic spots and neighbouring waterways around Chunchon Lake. Another point of interest in Chunchon is the **Koryo Silk Factory**, which offers the visitor close glimpses of this ancient oriental handicraft.

Beyond Chunchon are even more bucolic lakeside resorts. Due north, near Hwachon, is **Paro Lake**, which is generally less crowded than the Chunchon waterways. But the most scenic of all Korea's inland waterways is **Soyang Lake**, created by the Soyang Dam. On the north side of the dam there is a boat pier called Soyang Pavilion, and from here you may take leisurely boat tours on this lovely lake.

An interesting side-trip from Soyang Lake entails a 15-minute boat ride north from Soyang Pavilion and a 20-minute hike up a steep hillside from the dock. After passing a waterfall, you will come upon the **Chongpyong Temple**, a quiet Buddhist retreat founded about 1,600 years ago. This temple features colourfully painted beams and eaves, and especially fine murals on its outer walls.

For those who wish to get even further away, a trip northeast to the remote town of **Yanggu** is in order. It takes about 1.5 hours by shuttle-boat from the Soyang Pavilion. A bus or taxi will then take you from the dock into the town, which lies secluded in a beautiful wooded valley only a few miles from the DMZ. Yanggu is a typical Korean rural town, insulated from modern Western influences.

The next stop is the town of **Inje**, 32 kilometres (20 miles) east of Yanggu. If you have a car, drive yourself; otherwise use the public bus service. The road winds along riverbeds and mountain valleys until it reaches the Soyang River. Inje, which lies on the river's west bank, is the threshold to spectacular Mount Sorak National Park.

Mount Sorak: Snow-Peak Mountain

The third highest peak in Korea, Mount Sorak stands majestically in the midst of the Taebaek Sanmaek, the Great White Mountain Range. Part of this range, which dominates Korea's northeastern corner, has been designated as **Mount Sorak National Park**.

Overall, Sorak is the most scenic mountain park in Korea. Five square kilometres (two square miles) of Sorak Park, including a stretch of beach along the sea, have been blueprinted as an elaborate 'Leisure Land East', which will include such recreational facilities as hotels, campgrounds, hot-spring spas, ski slopes, hunting, fishing, water-skiing, additional trekking trails, tennis, golf and indoor sports.

The best season for scenery in Sorak is autumn, when forests of maple, oak and gingko set the mountains ablaze with fiery colours. Spring and summer are also quite lovely, especially for camping and long-distance hiking. Many people visit Sorak in winter to enjoy the mountain snowscapes, soak in hot mineral baths, and simply get away from crowded cities. Trails tend to be slippery and somewhat treacherous in the winter, but for rock-climbers it is the best time to scale Sorak's granite peaks in complete privacy.

If you are coming in from Chunchon via Inje, just continue driving east and soon you will enter Inner Sorak. You may also take a 40-minute flight from Seoul directly to Sokcho airport, then transfer to a bus or cab for the 30-minute ride into Outer Sorak. The fastest route by car or bus from Seoul is to follow the Yongdong Expressway directly to the eastern coastal town of Kangnung, then drive or take a local bus up to Sokcho and Outer Sorak. The express bus leaves for Kangnung every 20 minutes from Seoul's Kangnam Expressway Bus Terminal, and takes 3.5 hours at a cost of W1,500 one-way.

Inner Sorak

Inner Sorak remains relatively undeveloped and thus attracts experienced trekkers and mountain climbers who wish to escape totally all signs of civilization. The best approach is along the North Han River to Inje, after which the roads are unpaved and rather bumpy. From Inje, there are two routes into the Sorak Range: the northern route, which passes through the Chingpuryong and the Misilryong Passes and terminates at Sokcho, is the roughest and most remote. The southern route through the Hangyeryong Pass takes you to the coastal town of Yangyang and is the most scenic and convenient inland access to Sorak.

Favourite sights along the southern route to inner Sorak include the Taesung Falls — an easy hike up a trail from the roadside rest-stop

called Changsudae Villa — and the Paekdam Temple, a considerably longer and more difficult climb along the same trail. Further down the road towards the coast is another trail which leads up to the Yongdam Waterfall, the Pongjong-Am Hermitage and Taechong-Bong Peak, the highest peak in the Sorak Range at 1,708 metres (5630 feet). Be prepared for an arduous four- to six-hour trek up steep twisting trails, and bring along appropriate clothing, shoes, water and snacks, for here you will find few signs of civilization. Before you get to Yangyang, where marvellous seafood meals await the hungry hiker, stop off at the Osaek Yaksu Mineral Springs for a soothing hot soak.

Outer Sorak

Outer Sorak, only a few minutes' drive inland from the coastal town of Sokcho, is more developed for tourism and has comfortable hotels, inns, and recreational facilities. A well-maintained mountain park with craggy peaks and alpine scenery, Outer Sorak rivals anything in Switzerland or the western United States. **Sorak-dong**, the little resort village in the main valley, has a large youth hostel, numerous Korean inns and several comfortable deluxe hotels. A spacious park just beyond the village is the launching point for all hikes into Outer Sorak.

For those unable or unwilling to hike, there is a cable car carrying passengers from this base camp park all the way up to **Flying Fairy Peak (Pisondae)**. From this marvellous vantage point one may follow several trails to some of Sorak's most famous landmarks.

The primary cultural attraction in Outer Sorak is the **Sinhung Temple**, the world's oldest surviving Zen temple, originally built in AD 625. Destroyed by forest fire, it was rebuilt in 701. Destroyed by fire again, it was restored once more in 1645. The current structure was renovated in 1971 by Zen Buddhist monks. As you take the ten-minute stroll along a flagstone path from the park to the Sinhung Temple, note the little garden grottoes along the way, where bell-shaped tombstones mark the spots in which famous Buddhist monks have been buried over the centuries.

Some of Zen Buddhism's most eccentric characters are commemorated in the murals and icons of the Sinhung Temple. For example, the Chinese monks Han San and Sup Duk, known as the 'Two Crazy Idiots', are depicted grimacing grotesquely at the world on the temple's northern wall. On the rear wall of the main shrinehall, another Zen patriarch is depicted presenting his amputated arm as an offering to the famous Buddhist master Ta Mo (Bodhidharma).

Continue up the trail from Sinhung-sa to the Kejo Hermitage, another hour's hike uphill. Built into a granite cave, it houses a beautiful golden Buddha sitting in repose amid flickering candles and burning incense. A cool, narrow stone corridor leads you from the mouth of the cave into the inner sanctum. Across from the hermitage stands the famous Rolling Rock, a huge boulder perched precariously on the edge of a cliff. From here, trails wind even further up towards the granite peaks and, if you have the stamina, try to make it up to Ulsanbawi Rock, a craggy outcropping of granite 873 metres (2880 feet) high with breathtaking views of Sorak below and the East Sea in the distance.

Avid alpinists may trek up to Flying Fairy Peak, instead of using the cable car. From here, another hour of walking brings you to the famous Kumgang Cave, which affords superb mountain vistas. From the park below, yet another trail leads to Flying Dragon Waterfall (Piryong). To reach this waterfall, cross a swaying suspension bridge which hovers high above a narrow gorge and rushing mountain stream.

Accommodation

A good place to stay in Sorak is the new **Sorak Park Hotel**, a comfortable and tastefully designed hotel with a nightclub and casino for evening entertainment. The restaurant features Western, Korean and Japanese dishes, and two charming tearooms offer the visitor the opportunity to experience traditional Korean or Japanese tea ceremonies, using Sorak's pure mountain springwater.

Further up the road, adjacent to the base camp park, is the **Sorak Tourist Hotel**, an older establishment set in a shady grove, with very pleasant atmosphere and convenient access to all trails.

Taegu and the Haein Temple

In a broad plain 3.5 hours south of Seoul by express bus or train lies Taegu, Korea's third largest city, with a population of over one million. Striking a pleasant balance between urban and rural, modern and traditional elements, Taegu teems with Korean colour. It was on the northern outskirts of Taegu, at the Naktong River, that the initial communist onslaught which started the Korean War was stopped. Due to its location in an inland basin, Taegu is Korea's hottest city during the summer.

Taegu Sights

Taegu is the major market town for most of Korea's southern provinces. Its most famous product is apples, a fruit which was introduced to the area during the 19th century by the American missionary James Adams. Today, Taegu apples are prized throughout the Far East for their excellent flavour and fine texture. Visit the West Gate Market, one of Korea's oldest and most colourful food bazaars, for a close look at the incredible volume and variety of produce available.

Taegu is one of Korea's biggest herbal medicine markets. In **Yak-Chong Kol-Mok**, known to foreigners as 'medicine lane', an amazing assortment of gnarled wild plants, dried reptiles, bundles of poisonous insects and sundry parts of animals seldom seen by Western eyes are on public display.

Thirty minutes' drive north of the city is the Silla-era **Tonghwa Temple**, located on the steep slopes of Palgong Mountain. This temple sits serenely in a tranquil wooded glade, with the sounds of water rushing across boulder-strewn streambeds. There are many good hiking trails which lead to nearby hermitages.

Perched high in the mountains, 30 minutes' drive south of Taegu, is an exquisite little temple called **Yong-yon Temple**. The paintings of traditional Buddhist temple guardians which adorn Yong-yon-sa are especially beautiful. This too is an excellent hiking area, complete with clear mountain streams for *alfresco* bathing. Cosy little Korean inns provide overnight accommodation for those who wish to stay and explore for a while.

Taegu's daytime drabness and torpor give way to considerable sparkle and excitement at night. The town's nightlife is surprisingly colourful, and most of it is concentrated along Dong Sung Road, 'Taegu's Broadway'. The lanes of Dong Sung road are solidly lined with eating, drinking and entertainment establishments. The ambiance

of Dong Sung district is somewhat similar to Myong-dong in Seoul but it is far more local in character. Few foreign tourists are to be seen here.

The Haein Temple

Taegu can be fun for a day and a night, but the real reason for coming here is to visit one of Korea's most famous temples, the Haein Temple, located about an hour's drive west of Taegu in beautiful **Mt Kaya National Park**.

In AD 802, two monks named Sunung and Ich'ong made a holy pilgrimage to China. When they returned to Korea, they went into retreat in the forests of Mt Kaya. Soon afterwards, King Aejong's wife fell ill, but the court physicians could do nothing to save her. So he turned for help to these two monks, who were known throughout the realm for their purity and austerity. The monks effected a miraculous cure, and in his heartfelt gratitude the king built the Haein Temple for their use. *Haein* means an ocean so clear and calm that it reflects like a mirror — an ancient Buddhist symbol for mental tranquillity.

The Haein Temple complex consists of 50 major buildings, with 13 hermitages tucked into the nearby hills. The paintings on the walls of the gates and halls have unique blue-grey backgrounds and graphic images of Korean longevity and evil-repelling symbols, such as the Tiger, Dragon, Phoenix and Turtle. The temple's colour scheme of magenta, gold and blue blends beautifully with autumn colours.

In the central courtyard stands a fine triple-tiered pagoda and a stone lantern, both erected in the year 808. The Nine Lights Pavilion, which encloses the front side of the main courtyard, contains a small museum of Buddhist relics, including a fascinating self-portrait of a monk in the form of a life-size statue sitting in the lotus position.

A set of stone steps leads up to the main shrine wherein sits a gilt icon representing the Vairocana Buddha, the source of Buddha's enlightenment. Exquisite religious murals hang from ceiling to floor behind these seated gilt figures. To the left of the main shrine stands the Hall of Judgement, with images of the Ten Judges and graphic depictions of various Buddhist hells. On either side of the central courtyard are blocks of cells which serve as rooms for resident monks. The entire temple complex is under continuous renovation, utilizing stone and lumber taken from the mountains and employing the traditional skills of Korean craftsmen.

Buddha's Library Up the steep steps behind the main hall is the storehouse of the famous Tripitaka Koreana, Haein-sa's greatest claim to fame. Commissioned by King Kojong in 1236 during his long exile on Kanghwa Island during the Mongol occupation, the purpose of the mammoth project was to enlist the aid of Buddhist gods in ridding Korea of the Mongols. The text was based on the complete Chinese translation of the Buddhist Tripitaka, which was subsequently lost in China. Tripitaka means 'Three Baskets' and consists of *sutra* (discourse of Buddha's words), *viyana* (discipline, the rules of Buddhist practice) and *apidharma* (analysis; philosophical discussions about the sutra by renowned Buddhist scholars).

The white birch wood-blocks, each of which measures 24 centimetres (9.5 inches) wide, 74 centimetres (29 inches) long, and six centimetres (2.5 inches) thick, were imported from China and had to be seasoned for nine years: three years to soak in salt water, three years to dry in wind and shade and three more to dry in the sun. After that, 20 scribes and 180 wood carvers laboured for ten years to inscribe the complete Tripitaka on 80,000 of these wood-blocks, with no errors or deletions. Buddhist scholars from all over the world still visit the Haein Temple to study these ancient scriptures.

The library which houses the Tripitaka is the oldest building in the complex and dates from 1488. Two devasting fires which destroyed every other building in the complex left this library unscathed, a miracle attributed to divine protection. The library is ingeniously constructed. It lies at 750 metres (2475 feet), mid-way between sea level and the 1,500-metre (4,950-foot) summit of Mt Kaya.

Approach to Haein-sa beneath Autumn foliage.

Consequently, cold air from the mountain top and warm air from the valley floor meet and meld at this very point, which the monks located without the aid of altimeters or other modern devices. The library is thoroughly ventilated by a series of latticed windows of various sizes and angles to insure optimum circulation of air inside. Elevated shelves and deep troughs protect the collection against floods. Under the foundation lie thick layers of charcoal, lime, and salt, which absorb excess moisture during the humid summers and recycle it back into the library during the dry winters.

Apart from the main temple complex, there are many other scenic spots to visit in Mt Kaya National Park. The dense forests, lush valleys, rushing streams and sparkling waterfalls provide a pleasant background for the ancient Buddhist structures and cultural relics scattered throughout the hills.

Accommodation

A ten-minute walk up the road from the entrance to Mt Kaya Park and the Haein Temple is a little resort town where over a dozen Korean inns, numerous good restaurants, local bars, cafés and souvenir shops await the visitor. This is a pleasant place to spend a night or two, while exploring Haein-sa and Mt Kaya by day.

A particularly charming Korean inn, the **Kook Geh Inn**, overlooks the entire village from its cosy perch on a hilltop. Built entirely of wood in classical Korean style, you can't miss it if you walk up the hill behind the village. At a glance, it looks like a vision from another era. Each *ondol* room has sliding panel-doors and a painted folding screen inside to partition the room if necessary. Separate bathrooms and showers down the hall may be used privately.

The numerous little restaurants in this mountain village specialize in meals of wild mushrooms and other vegetables and herbs gathered in the surrounding wilderness.

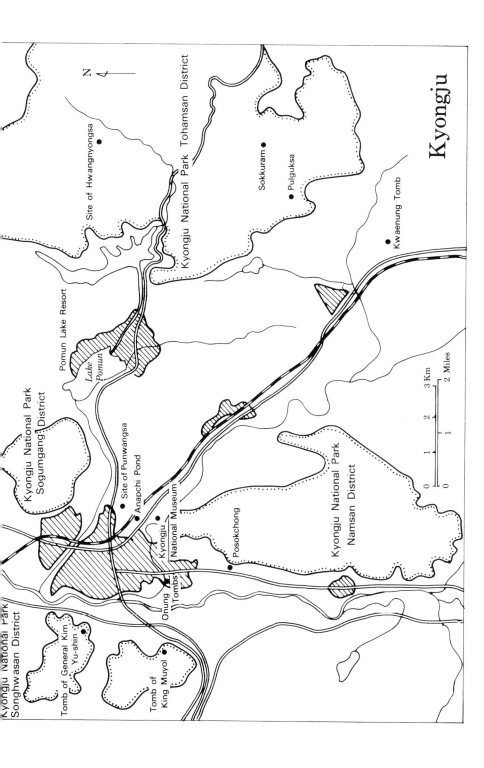

Kyongju

Kyongju: Valley of the Silla Kings

The Town

Kyongju lies in a valley some 70 kilometres (43 miles) west of Taegu. Entering the valley for the first time is like stepping into a time machine. It sweeps your imagination back 2,000 years for a grand tour of Korea's 'Golden Age' of culture, the Silla era, which lasted from 57 BC until AD 935 — only eight years short of a full millennium. Few of the world's great dynasties can boast such longevity. The cultural and political centre of this glorious dynasty was Kyongju. Here Silla kings reigned over one of the world's most advanced civilizations, traces of which remain scattered throughout the valley. Eclipsed for over 1,000 years when succeeding dynasties moved their capitals elsewhere, Kyongju has only recently awoken from its long slumber to rediscover its own ancient heritage. The treasures unearthed in the Kyongju Valley lie at the very core of Korea's current cultural renaissance.

The town itself is a typical, rather run-down Korean country town, with tree-lined streets and narrow bylanes. In the alleys directly across from the Kyongju train station there is a colourful open-air market with stalls displaying an exotic array of fresh seafoods, vegetables, fruits and other Korean culinary products. At the Silla Kiln you may purchase authentic reproductions of Silla pottery and statuary and observe master craftsmen at their trade.

The Valley of Tombs and Temples

For those interested in Oriental archaeology, history and art, Kyongju would be a wonderful place to spend a few weeks. The extensive resort facilities of Lake Pomun provide all sorts of healthy, outdoor recreation for relaxation, while the nearby hills and valleys contain endless treasure troves of ancient temples, burial mounds, palace ruins, Buddhist statuary and other fascinating relics which span the entire thousand-year history of Silla. It would take several weeks of thorough exploration to do Kyongju full justice, but described below are the main highlights, which may be covered in two or three days.

Tumuli Park The burial ground of King Michu (reigned AD 262–83) and at least 20 other Silla kings, this park — which lies just to the south of City Hall, in downtown Kyongju — was created in 1973, when 180 encroaching village dwellings were razed and the entire area was enclosed and landscaped. Note the many stands of juniper, pine and bamboo planted throughout the park, some of which cover entire burial mounds. These ancient symbols of longevity always appear in Korean burial grounds. The mounds themselves vary in size: if the

ruler was good, the people buried him in a big mound; if he was inept
or incapable, he was interned in a small mound.

Since its opening in 1973, Tumuli Park has turned up 11,526
priceless cultural relics, which are now on display in national museums
of Kyongju and Seoul. Most of these artefacts came from the Tomb of
the Heavenly Horse, the only one of the 20 burial chambers to be
excavated so far. One can only imagine how much more lies buried
beneath the ground. Tourists may enter the Cheonma (Heavenly
Horse) Tomb, where replicas of the most precious items found there
are displayed in wall niches. Due to the acidity of Korea's soil, even
the bones of the deceased king have long since disintegrated, but his
solid gold crown, his belt of beaten gold, jade ornaments and other
personal possessions were found intact in their original positions when
the tomb was opened.

One should note carefully the Silla royal crown, which is surely one
of the most unique crowns in the world. The three tall structures at the
front of the crown represent cosmic pine trees, and the two at the back
represent reindeer antlers — both are important symbols of longevity
as well as ancient signs of shaman power. The entire crown is adorned
with comma-shaped pendants of pure jade, which represent the claws
of the tiger, the most potent repeller of evil influences. Every bit as
precious and ornate as European or Chinese crowns, the crowns worn
by Silla kings display the additional sophistication of profound
philosophical symbolism.

Tomb of King Muyol About five minutes' drive from town lies a
spectacular group of tombs collectively referred to as King Muyol's
Tomb. King Muyol, who conquered the rival Paekche Kingdom and
paved the way for his successor King Munmu to complete the job of
unifying Korea, is memorialized by an impressive monument just
inside the gate. On a large stone tortoise sits a heavy capstone covered
with intricately carved dragons, symbolizing his royal power. The path
beyond the wooded area around the tomb affords splendid views of
four more burial mounds standing against a background of open sky
and rolling hills.

Tomb of General Kim Yu-Shin General Kim Yu-shin was one of
Korea's outstanding military heroes. Along with King Muyol, whose
armies he led during Silla's seventh-century campaigns to unify Korea's
Three Kingdoms, he is regarded as one of the 'Three Unifiers' and a
founding father of the Korean nation.

Though smaller than King Muyol's tomb, the tomb of General Kim
displays a far greater sophistication in design. Encircled by a host of
superbly carved figures from the Oriental zodiac, the tomb lies on a
wooded bluff overlooking the Kyongju Valley.

Onung Tombs To the south of town lie five of Silla's most ancient tombs, including the tomb of the king who founded Silla 2,000 years ago, in 57 BC. Here one finds several shrines erected in honour of the founding king, who is said to have been born on this very spot from a golden egg left by a horse which flew down from heaven. Hidden in a clump of pine and bamboo is another shrine dedicated to Silla's first queen, who is reported to have been born from the rib of a dragon, as Eve was sprung from Adam's rib.

Kwaenung Tomb Twelve kilometres (seven miles) south of town lies the quiet and seldom visited Kwaenung Tomb, the mound of which is entirely encircled by exquisitely carved stone reliefs depicting the twelve animals of the Oriental zodiac. Rows of stone statues which guard the approach to the tomb make this site even more unique. Military officers, civil officials, lions and monkeys stand in perpetual vigil before the tomb of their royal master. The wavy hair, heavy beards and prominent noses of the military figures probably represent facial features of the Persian mercenaries who are known to have served the Silla court.

Pulguk Temple Founded in 528 by a minister of the Silla court, the Pulguk Temple was expanded to present proportions in 751. It was destroyed by rampaging Japanese troops in 1593, and in 1970 work began to restore the entire complex to its original form, a project completed in 1972. Pulguk-sa is a perfect example of how faithful and true to traditional form the Koreans have been in renovating their ancient temples.

The entire complex is built into a wooded glade where groves of pine and juniper have been carefully cultivated. The various halls, pavilions and shrines are located in walled compounds which rise in ascending levels up the hillside. From the top, the temple roofs form a 'sea' of tile as you gaze across them. In the main courtyard stand two large pagodas which are considered to be the best surviving examples of classical Silla masonry in Korea. The more ornate Tabotop Pagoda represents the ascent of man from an unrefined state to the purity and perfection of Buddhist enlightenment, symbolized by the round lotus motif at the top. Across the courtyard stands the strong, masculine Sokkatap Pagoda, which symbolizes man's descent into the earthly realm. Both are over 1,000 years old.

In the main prayer hall sits a large gilt Buddha. Up the steep steps behind the main hall, in the top corner of the complex, is a lovely little shrinehall dedicated to Guan Yin, Goddess of Mercy. This hall is a particularly graceful and compact example of traditional Korean temple architecture at its very best. Its perfect proportions and subtle harmony evoke the sublime serenity associated with monastic life.

The Sokkuram Buddha Up the road from Pulguk-sa, high on a mountain summit, is Sokkuram, the Cave of the Stone Buddha. Once it required a long hard climb up steep mountain paths to get there. Today a paved road winds all the way up to the top. From the parking lot, a wooded path twists several hundred metres along a steep ridge to the shrine.

In the lower courtyard, a Fountain of Youth trickles into a broad granite basin. It is said that a cup of this pure mountain water will prolong life by ten years. Off to the side is a small hermitage where resident monks live and work. A set of stone steps takes you up the final ascent to the Sokkuram grotto.

On a lotus dais inside a large man-made cave of huge granite slab is a reposing figure which most Oriental art historians regard as the most aesthetically perfect, sublimely tranquil image of Sakyamuni Buddha ever executed by man. A marvel of classical beauty, graceful form and perfect proportion, this white-granite statue of Buddha sits in serenity facing due east towards the rising sun. Even children are awed and silenced by the sight. Nothing in India, China or Japan approaches the power and beauty radiated by this image, yet only in recent years has Korea's importance as a repository of genuine Buddhist learning and art come to light.

The cave forms an organic, harmoniously balanced grotto. The entrance hall is guarded by eight heroic generals in stone relief and two wild-looking guardians standing in classical martial-arts poses. Four Deva Kings protect the inner portal. In a circle around the Buddha are relief images of the Ten Great Disciples and the Eight Great Bodhisattvas. Due to the great number of tourists who now come to see the Sokkuram Buddha, visitors must view the well-lit grotto from behind a glass partition.

Bunhwang-Sa Pagoda This small temple boasts the oldest surviving pagoda in Korea. Built in AD 634 under the auspices of Silla's Queen Sondok, the pagoda displays superb relief carvings and guardian statues. Originally nine stories high, the three surviving tiers are built entirely of stones cut to the size of bricks. In the courtyard is another Fountain of Youth, and whether or not the water adds decades to one's life, it certainly tastes as pure and fresh as water can be. A 1,300-year-old gilt Buddha graces the main prayer hall, and the grounds are beautifully landscaped with flowering fruit trees, pine and juniper, bamboo and weeping willows.

Other Sights

In addition to tombs and temples, the Kyongju Valley abounds with other cultural relics and archaeological sites. In a hillside grove of pine, for example, stand the three mysterious statues known as the **Triple Buddhas**. First discovered lying askew on the slopes of nearby Namsan in 1923, these statues reflect none of the stylistic characteristics of classical Silla statuary. Instead, they show the massive proportions and bold lines of the Koguryo style far to the north. No one knows how they got to the Kyongju Valley. Today they are kept in a walled grotto and tended by a family.

Posokdong Bower was once the site of an elaborate Silla pleasure palace. All that remains today is a granite trough shaped somewhat like an abalone, which is what 'Posok' means. Set in a shaded glade, this trough used to be the site of drunken revelries. The king with his entourage of courtiers and concubines would sit around the stone waterway while dancers performed in the middle. Suddenly, the king would blurt out a line of poetry and command one of his courtiers to come up with an appropriate matching line. At the same time, he would set a large cup of wine afloat in the trough, and if the chosen courtier had not produced an acceptable line by the time the cup reached him, he had to drink it bottoms up.

Anapchi Pond was also the site of royal pleasure pavilions, where Silla kings fished for carp, went boating with concubines and composed verse in absolute tranquillity. It was constructed in 674 under the auspices of King Munmu to celebrate the unification of Korea under the Silla banner. The original layout of the park was contrived as a miniature version of the United Silla Kingdom, complete with rivers and mountains, seas and lagoons, pavilions and palaces. It was here in 935 that the last Silla king finally surrendered to invading forces, bringing the 1,000 year-old Silla Dynasty to an end. Repaired and landscaped in 1975, Anapchi Pond is now a pleasant park with echoes still of the grandeur and luxury enjoyed by Silla royalty.

The **Kyongju Museum**, an elegant contemporary structure with the stylish flair of classical Korean architecture, houses the priceless collection of Silla artefacts unearthed from the tombs, temples and other historical sites throughout the Kyongju Valley. Of special interest are the solid gold ornaments with which Silla kings bedecked themselves.

In a separate pavilion outside the museum hangs the famous **Emille Bell** (pronounced 'emil-leh'), one of the largest, most resonant in Asia. Cast over a thousand years ago by royal command, the bell had a sad birth. According to the story, the bell maker tried repeatedly to cast the bell according to the king's specifications, but each time it split with the first resounding ring. Distraught and shamed by his failure, he was on the verge of committing suicide when an old monk appeared and told his own widowed sister that her brother's task could be accomplished and his own life saved only through the sacrifice of her infant daughter. At first horrified but finally unable to resist his sister's entreaties, the desperate bell maker took the baby girl to his workshop one day and threw her into the molten metal. When the bell was cast and completed, not only did it ring without cracking, it emitted a mournful undertone reminiscent of a child crying for her mother, which in the ancient Silla language was pronounced 'emil-leh'. Whether true or not, this story is an interesting reflection of the deep shamanist roots which have always remained hidden just below the surface of Korean culture, even after the introduction of Buddhism, which obviously would never countenance human sacrifice.

Travellers with sufficient time and interest may venture even further off the beaten track by visiting Pagoda Valley, Buddha Valley, T'ap Valley, Kuksa Valley or the more remote Sungbang Valley, all of which lie within driving distance of Kyongju. New discoveries are unearthed every year in and around the Kyongju Valley, and ideally every visit to Korea should include a few days there to view the latest treasures.

Accommodation and Resort Facilities

Considered Korea's 'museum without walls', Kyongju is also rapidly becoming a major international resort. The **Lake Pumon Resort**, set around a large artificial lake about 20 minutes' drive from town, currently boasts four deluxe hotels, and ten more are planned.

Among Lake Pumon's hotels, the Silla-style **Kyongju Chosun** provides the most pleasant atmosphere and service. Spacious, comfortable, and tastefully appointed with wood furnishings, the Kyongju Chosun has a traditional air which blends well with its historic setting.

For those who wish to steep themselves entirely in Korean atmosphere, the best place to stay is at one of the traditional inns at the little resort town adjacent to the Pulguk Temple. Constructed entirely in ancient Silla style, this tourism centre has numerous shops, cafés and restaurants, as well as over a dozen thoroughly traditional *yogwan* (Korean inns), each with its own personality.

By night in Kyongju, you may dance to the latest tunes at one of the hotel disco clubs, or try your luck at the casino in the **Kolon Hotel**. For a thoroughly delightful cultural experience, try an evening at **Yo Suk Gung**, a charming establishment which combines traditional

Korean restaurant, *kisaeng* and entertainment services under one classical roof.

Kyongju is pleasant all year round, but the best time to go is in autumn, when the annual Silla Cultural Festival is held from 8 to 10 October. The entire valley reverberates with parades, Buddhist rites, farmers' bands, music and dance, folk games, and colourful pageantry commemorating great historical events.

Getting to Kyongju

To get to Kyongju from Seoul, one has three choices: take the 55-minute Korean Airlines flight to Taegu, then transfer to a bus for the hour-long ride to Kyongju; take the Saemaul super-express train from the Seoul Railway Station for a pleasant 4.5-hour ride through the Korean countryside directly to Kyongju; or grab an express bus from Seoul's Kangnam Expressway Bus Terminal, where buses leave every hour from 7 am to 6 pm and make the trip to Kyongju along the scenic Seoul-Pusan Expressway in 4.5 hours. Of course, the best way to go is to rent a car and drive yourself. A private car would come in very handy when visiting the far-flung cultural sites scattered throughout the valley.

From Pusan, Kyongju-bound express buses leave every half hour from 6 am until 8 pm from Pusan's Express Bus Terminal. The ride takes one hour 40 minutes. A shuttle bus also runs regularly from Pusan's Kimhae Airport directly to the Lake Pumon Resort. The most interesting way to travel between Kyongju and Pusan in either direction is by steam locomotive, a recently renovated service which departs daily from Pusan at 9.30 am and returns daily from Kyongju at 1.10 pm. The three-hour ride costs about W2,000. The engine is a genuine antique steam locomotive complete with billowing black smoke, screeching steam-whistle and old-fashioned fittings. The cars have been entirely refurbished and luxuriously appointed with comfortable seats, heating and cooling systems, tasteful decor and a dining car.

If you arrive in Kyongju without your own car and without an organized tour group, rest assured that there is a wide range of day tours available in Kyongju for 'FIT's' (foreign individual travellers). The simplest one is a 1.5-hour tour of Pulguk Temple and the Sokkuram Grotto. The most extensive is a full-day tour of 15 major sites. Contact the information desk of any deluxe hotel in the area or the Kyongju Information Centre for details.

Pusan: Seaport and Beach Resort

With three million residents, Pusan is Korea's second largest city and its principal international seaport. Like Seoul, it is designated as a 'Special City', which means that it is administered directly by the central government rather than by provincial authorities. Situated in a depression of land surrounded by hills, Pusan is sometimes referred to as a 'cauldron' (Pusan literally means 'cauldron mountain'). Industry and commerce dominate the downtown areas, but there are some good resorts and interesting sights within the immediate vicinity of Pusan.

City Sights

The **United Nations Cemetery** is in the southeastern part of the city. Here lie the bodies of soldiers from the 16 nations which fought together under UN command to defend South Korea during the Korean War. Christian crosses of European nations sit alongside the Islamic crescents of the Turkish brigade. In the central plaza fly the flags of all sixteen nations.

On a steep slope facing the sea is a park called **Yongdu-San** (Dragon Head Mountain), which commands superb views of downtown Pusan and the harbour. It is a good place to go for strolls or simply to relax and get away from the urban clamour of downtown Pusan. For even more magnificent views, ascend the Pusan Tower, a tall TV transmission tower set in the middle of the park with an observation deck at the top.

Among the most colourful sights in downtown Pusan is the **Fish Market**, located in the centre of town, where the fishing boats dock. There is a truly exotic array of fresh fish and molluscs from the East Sea, with many varieties unfamiliar to Western eyes.

A 20-minute drive from the downtown district out to the tip of Yongdo Island brings you to **Taejongdae Park**, where King Muyol used to come for rest and recuperation after his battles to unify Korea. It overlooks the sea and the entrance to Pusan harbour. The park is currently under intensive development as a tourist resort, and will soon have many recreational facilities to entertain visitors to Pusan.

The ornate palatial building which dominates the downtown skyline is the **Commodore Dynasty Hotel**, a worthy city sight in itself. Set on a landscaped hilltop, this colourful hotel is a convenient place to stay in downtown Pusan. Its style is somewhat reminiscent of the Grand Hotel in Taipei. Near the entrance is an interesting replica of Admiral Yi's famous Turtle Ships, the world's first armour-plated warships.

Hot Springs and Beach Resorts

In addition to having Korea's major seaport, Pusan has one of the country's most popular beach resorts. Not far from city hall and Yongdusan Park is **Songdo Beach**, an inexpensive but often crowded local resort. The beach itself is clean, but the water lies a bit too close to the murky waters of the harbour.

The most pleasant Pusan beach resort for international travellers lies 18 kilometres (12 miles) northeast of town. At the **Haeundae Beach Resort** there are several modern hotels, including the deluxe **Chosun Beach Hotel**, one of the best hotels in Korea. The long, curving beach is lapped by clean waters and is perfect for swimming. There are also hot springs and medicinal bathhouses for those who prefer therapeutic bathing to beach bathing.

Fourteen kilometres (nine miles) north of downtown Pusan is the region's oldest mineral spa, the **Tongnae Hot Springs**, known since the late 19th century for its rejuvenating waters. Two tourist hotels and several local inns provide cosy accommodation; all are equipped with mineral baths fed by natural hot springs.

Side Trips

A few kilometres north of Tongnae Hot Springs, on the eastern slopes of Mt Kumjong, sits **Pomo Temple**, headquarters of the Dyana Sect. The final approach to this elegant temple, founded in AD 678, crosses a graceful stone bridge over a musical mountain stream. Three attractive temple gates give access to the main complex. The temple grounds are landscaped in classical fashion, with stands of Korea's favourite trees gracefully placed here and there and genuine Silla relics such as pagodas and stone lanterns subtly positioned for maximum aesthetic effect.

A little further away is the **Tongdo Temple**, a lovely site seldom visited by tourists. It is located halfway between Pusan and Kyongju along the Seoul-Pusan Expressway, and has its own clearly marked exit. With a total of 65 structures, Tongdo-sa ranks as Korea's largest temple, and almost every Buddhist deity is honoured there with his individual shrine. The architecture of this temple complex reflects various styles from different eras of Korean history. The main hall, for example, is T-shaped rather than square or rectangular. The main entrance is guarded by four massive Deva kings, and the temple walls display excellent samples of Buddhist painting. Tongdo-sa was founded in 646 by a Korean scholar who had travelled to China in search of a true faith which would benefit the Korean nation. On his return, he founded this temple in order to preserve the learning and experience he brought back from China.

Pusan is also a popular launching point for side trips by boat, with ferries to the Hallyo Waterway, Cheju Island and Shimonoseki, Japan.

Getting to Pusan

From Seoul, Korean Airlines runs eight flights a day to Pusan and flight time is 50 minutes. Express trains to Pusan make the trip in 4.5 hours and leave Seoul six times a day. Express buses, which take six hours, depart Seoul for Pusan every 10 minutes. From Kyongju, express bus and train service to Pusan takes about 45 minutes. A recently renovated steam locomotive goes to Pusan once a day in three hours' time, but the best route is by car.

The East Side: Coastal Resorts and Mountain Retreats

Stretching 390 scenic kilometres (240 miles) from Hwajinpo Beach, just below the DMZ, down to Pohang, Korea's east coast has some of the country's most spectacular seascapes. A region of many contrasts, the rugged eastern coastline is punctuated by deep ravines and prominent pine-bluffs, quiet fishing coves and lovely inland lagoons. The clear blue water and clean white sand form some of Korea's best swimming beaches. Pavilions for gazing at the rising sun or setting moon are located on wooded promontories along the entire length of the coast. Only a few minutes' drive inland are scenic mountain parks and hot spring spas.

The logical place to begin a trip down the east coast is Mt Sorak National Park. Otherwise, take the Yongdong Expressway from Seoul to **Kangnung**, then travel north along the coast road to **Sokcho**, which is the northernmost town of any significant size on the east coast. Express buses run regularly from Seoul to Kangnung in about 3.5 hours, and from there local buses will take you up to Sokcho. However, the best way to see the east coast is by private car. Indeed, a leisurely drive down Korea's east coast is one of the most scenic in the entire Far East.

About half an hour before reaching Kangnung, on the southern side of the Yongdong Expressway, is the **Dragon Valley**, Korea's best ski resort, located just eight kilometres (five miles) from the expressway. Scenic in all seasons, Dragon Valley is a good place to stop for lunch en route to the east coast.

Travelling south from Sokcho, the next major town is **Yang-yang**. En route one passes the **Uisangdae Pavilion**, named after the monk Uisang, who liked to stroll there. Pavilions such as this, set high on coastal pine-bluffs overlooking the sea, are dotted along this coastline, and early risers visit them to view the sunrise.

A little south of the pavilion is the **Naksan Temple**, built by the monk Uisang in AD 671. On the sea side of the main hall stands Naksan-sa's most famous attraction: a 16-metre (53-foot) white granite statue of Buddhism's most popular Bodhisattva, Kwanseum (Gwanyin in China, Avalokitesvara in India), more commonly known as the Goddess of Mercy. Here fishing families gather to pray for the safe return of their fleets.

The story of this statue is interesting. In 1972, Choe Won-chol, chief monk of Naksan Temple, had a dream in which an old monk appeared as an apparition and told him to build this statue, explaining exactly where to place it and how to construct it. He reported his strange dream to the headquarters of the Chogye Sect in Seoul, and after due consideration the elders decided to proceed with the project.

Drive through Yang-yang and continue down the coast until you see the sign for **Hajodae Pavilion**. Located on another beautiful pine-covered promontory, this pavilion offers superb views of the eastern coastline with its blue water, white sand, and green hills rolling into the horizon. Nearby is **Hajodae Beach**, a good place to stop for a swim.

Continuing south, you will soon see the sign for **Mt Odae National Park** pointing inland. The region around 1,563-metre (5160-foot) high Mt Odae is dotted with old hermitages, meditation retreats, Silla artefacts, and two famous temples, Woljong-sa and Sangwon-sa. Along the roads and paths to both of these temples are numerous shrines and memorials dedicated to famous monks, as well as large, bell-shaped granite tombstones marking the spots where great Buddhist masters are buried.

Moon-Gazing Lake and Beach Resort

Kangnung is a quiet fishing town rich in local colour and traditional architecture. The annual Tano Spring Festival is held here on the fifth day of the fifth month of the lunar calendar (usually in May). It continues for a full week. This is the best time to visit — otherwise, there is little of interest to the tourist.

The place to go is the **Kyongpodae Beach Resort**, just a few kilometres north of Kangnung proper. There are several seaside tourist hotels here, including the cosy, old-fashioned **Kyongpodae Tourist Hotel** and the larger **Donghae** (East Sea) **Hotel**, which sits on a landscaped hillside overlooking the sea. The hotels lie between the beach and a large glassy lake which used to serve Korean noblemen and their ladies as a vast reflecting mirror while they sat in elegant pavilions for moon-gazing along its grassy banks. The beach itself is clean and quiet, the water cool and bracing.

One of Kyongpodae's biggest attractions is a row of Korean seafood restaurants located just down the street from the Kyongpodae Tourist Hotel.

The Coast Road

From Kangnung, the drive south has been graded and paved to form a flawless black ribbon which winds all the way down to the southern coast. This part of the drive is highly reminiscent of California's scenic highway between Monterey and Big Sur, with its fabulous shorelines and rugged mountains dropping abruptly down to the sea. Allowing

Old men playing cards, their hanbok *immaculately laundered. The cards represent natural objects.*

135

plenty of time for leisurely stops along the way, the drive to Pohang — where the coast road terminates — takes about a day, so it is best to start out from Kangnung early in the morning.

The first point of interest south of Kangnung is the **Jugseo-Ru Pavilion**, located just off the road in the little town of Sancheong. It was built in 1275 as a pleasure pavilion for gazing at the moon, a favourite Korean pastime.

As soon as you pass the exits for Ulchin, look for the sign to the **Sugryu Limestone Cave**, surely one of Korea's most exotic natural formations. Four hundred and seventy metres (1550 feet) deep, this natural limestone cave was formed 250 million years ago and rivals even the most elaborate Walt Disney fantasy for bizarre effects. The entire cave is convoluted with strange stalactites, stalagmites and other rock formations, which over the centuries have acquired such colourful names as 'Maitreya Buddha', 'Cloud Rock', 'A Nymph's Secret Room', and the obviously phallic 'Love Ball', which hangs suggestively over a placid pool called Dragon Pond, one of five natural ponds inside the cave. The Chinese juniper growing near the cave's narrow entrance is about 1,000 years old. The entrance fee is nominal, and the entire interior is floodlit.

Health enthusiasts will enjoy a stop at the **Paekam Mineral Springs**, ten kilometres (six miles) inland along a newly paved road, about 40 kilometres (25 miles) south of Ulchin. The drive cuts through typical Korean farmlands and is very scenic.

The next scenic spot en route to Pohang is Mount Chuwang National Park. You can get there via the coastal town of Yongdok, which is famous for its fresh 'Yongdok Crab'. It is best to drive yourself or hire a cab, for the public bus ride can be rather jolting. Chuwang is a range of tall granite peaks, deep abrupt gorges, and remote mountain hermitages. One finds few visitors here.

Halfway between Yongdok and Pohang is the **Pogyong Temple**, an ancient temple with the quintessential ambiance of traditional Buddhist monastic life. The temple is surrounded by magnificent mountain scenery, and a short hike will bring you to a pool formed by one of the 11 waterfalls in the area. In summer, this is a great place for refreshing dips in bracing mountain waters. The temple, like most in Korea, dates from the ancient Silla era. A pleasant local *yogwan* (Korean inn) provides comfortable accommodation for those wishing to stay overnight.

Pohang and Points Beyond

As you approach Pohang, you cannot miss it. It stains the sky yellow and grey with industrial fumes. A port city as well as one of Korea's most important centres of heavy industry, Pohang's pride and joy is the **Pohang Iron and Steel Co**, Korea's first integrated steel mill, which currently rolls out 8.5 million tons of crude steel per year, both for export and domestic use. If you like the spectacle of huge blazing blast furnaces, pools of molten ore being cast into moulds and associated sights, you may arrange tours of this impressive steel mill through the public relations department.

There are two beaches around Pohang, **Pohang Beach** and **Kuryongpo Beach**. But the main reason for stopping in Pohang is to catch the Han Il Ho express ferry out to **Ullung Island**.

The next point of interest beyond Pohang is Kyongju, a 45-minute drive southwest of Pohang along an expressway.

The West Side: Mountains, Temples and the Paekche Legacy

Prior to its defeat by the combined forces of Silla and Tang China in AD 660, the ancient Paekche Kingdom held domain over the western plains and the west coast region of Korea. While Korea's east coast is renowned mainly for its beautiful seashores and magnificent natural scenery, the west side is most famous for Paekche cultural relics, mountain parks and old temples.

The west side of Korea is currently under intensive development to accommodate Korea's ever growing tourist industry. Interest in the west side has been greatly enhanced by the discovery in recent years of important cultural artefacts dating from the Paekche era, whose culture had an enormous influence on the early formation of Japanese civilization. Therefore, emphasis is being placed on the reconstruction of important historical sites, especially around Puyo and Kongju. These two towns were to Paekche what Kyongju was to Silla, and every year remarkable new discoveries are being unearthed in this ancient archaeological treasure trove.

Onyang

A good place to begin a west side tour is the popular hot springs resort of Onyang, less than an hour's drive south of Seoul. To get there, take the Seoul-Pusan Expressway south as far as Chonan, then exit west onto Highway 21, and follow the road 18 kilometres (11 miles) out to Onyang.

Onyang is a pleasant resort town, popular among honeymooners without the time or money to venture to more distant destinations. It has many hotels and inns, all of which are equipped with natural hot spring baths and offer professional massages. There is enough to do and see in Onyang to justify an overnight stay, but even if one is just passing through, it is well worth stopping long enough for a rejuvenating mineral bath and a relaxing massage.

Since 1978, Onyang's main attraction has been the **Onyang Folk Museum**, a private museum built and owned by Kim Won-dae. The 7,000 authentic Korean folk artefacts displayed here all come from his private collection, and they comprise the greatest exhibit of its kind in Korea. There are also three diorama exhibit halls which re-create traditional Korean folk life in vivid and convincing detail.

Onyang's other great attraction is the **Hyonchung-Sa Shrine**, an extensive memorial park in honour of the great naval hero Admiral Yi, who was born and raised here. First erected by King Sukjong in 1704,

it fell into disrepair after 1910, when Japan occupied Korea and tried to suppress all forms of Korean nationalism. It was re-opened by President Park on 28 April 1969, on the anniversary of Admiral Yi's birth, which has been celebrated here ever since with a colourful festival.

The elegant, dignified shrine to Admiral Yi sits high on a hillside overlooking this spacious and exquisitely landscaped park, one of the loveliest in Korea. There is also a museum of relics, including the tomb of Yi's favourite son — who died defending the family home against the Japanese.

Beaches and Exotic Flora

From Onyang, one heads westward into the scenic Kaya Hills towards Sosan, gateway to the Taean Peninsula. Halfway there, the **Sudok Temple** is perched high on the southern slope of Mt Toksung. A rather arduous climb above this temple leads to a large Maitreya Buddha carved into the face of the mountain.

Due west from Sosan is the town of **Taean**, the last major bus terminus for this portion of the west coast. Taean is within easy reach of three beaches and a scenic island, all of which are part of the **Sosan Seashore National Park**. To the south lies **Anmyon Island**, a beautiful offshore isle covered with unusual flora. To the west is **Mallipo Beach**, one of Korea's finest swimming resorts, complete with comfortable lodging facilities and over three kilometres (two miles) of clean sandy beach.

A little to the north of Mallipo lies **Chollipo Beach**, another paradise for fanciers of exotic flora. Of interest here is the famous **Chollipo Arboretum**, a project initiated in 1970 by Carl Ferris Miller, an American who has resided in Korea for over 40 years and is a naturalized Korean citizen. Over 6,000 domestic and imported species are cultivated at this arboretum, including the rarest members of the magnolia family, the world's best collection of ilex, exceptional samples of daphne and berberis, 40 species of Asian maple, and 450 types of hybridized holly.

On the coast just below Anmyon Island is one of Seoul's favourite beach resorts, located 14 kilometres (8.5 miles) from the town of **Taechon** amid one of Korea's lushest agricultural basins. Indeed, the entire western plain is often described as Korea's rice bowl.

Taechon Beach is divided into a Korean beach to the north and a foreigners beach to the south. The Korean beach is lined with numerous inns and wine-houses and remains lively day and night during the peak summer season. The foreigner's beach, which used to be the exclusive summer resort of Christian missionaries, is

considerably more peaceful and quiet. Today, international
businessmen and bankers from Seoul, as well as missionary families,
still maintain villas and bungalows at Taechon Beach, and tourists may
arrange to rent these for brief holidays by inquiring with residents of
Taechon town.

Puyo, Kongju and the Paekche Legacy

To get to Puyo and Kongju from Taean, it is best to return to the
Seoul-Pusan Expressway, then exit again further south at Chongju and
follow Highway 36 out to Kongju. From Taechon, one can negotiate
local country roads directly across to Kongju.

Kongju was the first capital of the Paekche Kingdom (AD
200−700). In 1971, workers digging a drainage ditch stumbled upon
the tomb of King Munyong, who ruled Paekche between 501 and 523.
Most of Paekche's royal tombs have long since been looted and left in
ruins but when excavated, this tomb revealed over 3,000 valuable
Paekche artefacts, which are now on display at the **Kongju National
Museum**. The style and motifs of these artefacts clearly reflect the
formative influence which Paekche culture exerted on Japanese
civilization.

Fifty kilometres (31 miles) southwest of Kongju along scenic
Highway 23 lies **Puyo**, Paekche's second capital. Rich in Paekche
legends and cultural relics, Puyo is rapidly becoming a major tourist
destination. The **Puyo National Museum**, one of Korea's most original
architectural wonders, houses prehistoric implements found in the
area, as well as cultural artefacts from Paekche times. Designed
according to classical Paekche proportions and style, this museum has
been publicly criticized in Korea for appearing 'too Japanese'.
Ironically, the Puyo Museum faithfully recreates an indigenous
Paekche style of building which was adopted intact by the Japanese
during the seventh to ninth centuries. This style subsequently disappeared in Korea, but the Japanese maintained it down to the present
century, which accounts for the misguided criticism and provides
further evidence of Paekche's indelible influence on Japanese art and
architecture.

In a spacious park set on a steep hill in the middle of Puyo is the
site where the last king of Paekche made his final stand against
invading armies from Tang China. Among the many pavilions and
historical relics preserved in this park, the most dramatic sight is the
Falling Flowers Cliff, a steep rock promontory overlooking the placid
waters of the White Horse River far below. According to the legend,
as the Chinese General Su Ting-fang was poised over the river to make
his final assault on Paekche, 3,000 palace ladies in full court attire

proceeded to this cliff and hurled themselves en masse into the river below, preferring death to dishonour at the hands of foreign soldiers. As they fell, their colourful silk skirts billowed out, suggesting the image of falling flowers. A pavilion in honour of their sacrifice stands vigil at the top of the cliff.

Facing east stands the **Yongilru** (Sun-Greeting) **Pavilion**, where the last Paekche king is said to have witnessed what he knew would be his last sunrise. Facing west is the **Songwoldae** (Moon-Watching) **Pavilion**, where he kept vigil and gazed at the moon the night before his final battle. Further down the hill is the Samchung-Sa Shrine, erected in honour of three great Paekche heroes. A colourful ceremony is held at this shrine every October, during Puyo's annual Paekche Cultural Festival, which is the best time to visit Puyo.

The town of Puyo itself is pleasant and quiet, with an interesting maze of lanes in the centre of town where the local markets, restaurants and taverns are located. The place to stay is the new **Puyo Youth Hostel**. Don't be misled by the name, for in addition to group facilities for youngsters, this hotel has deluxe private rooms for tourists, a coffee shop, a dining hall, and even a swimming pool. The White Horse River flows just down the street, and the hilltop park stands behind the hostel.

Leaving Puyo for points further south, drive southwest along Highway 23 to **Nonsan**, near which are the **Kwanchok** (Candlelight) **Temple** and Korea's largest solid stone Buddha, the Unjin Miruk, or Buddha of the Future.

Chonju: Paper and *Pi Pim Pap*

Halfway between Taejon and Kwangju, 93 kilometres (58 miles) south of Seoul, is the quaint town of **Chonju**, famous for paper and *pi pim pap*.

Chonju is the ancestral home of the Yi clan, which founded Korea's last dynasty in 1392, but today it is most famous for food and paper products. Papercraft was introduced to Korea from China about 1,000 years ago, and the craftsmen of Chonju still employ traditional methods and materials to produce some of the finest paper in the Orient. Raw materials include mulberry, bamboo, the thang tree, bark chips and even algae. Handmade Korean paper is greatly prized among Chinese and Japanese calligraphers and painters. You can observe the paper-making process from start to finish at **Oh Dong-Ho's Paper Factory**, located at the end of Chonju's main street near the city's ancient south gate (Pungnam-mun).

Chonju is also one of Korea's great gourmet centres, and it specializes in a Korean culinary delight called *pi pim pap*. You can try

Barbershops and Bathhouses

Barbershops and bathhouses in Korea are more than just places to get a haircut and a wash. They are venerable social institutions which provide the harried worker or businessman with a relaxing hour or two of pampered luxury. This is a grand tradition throughout the Orient, but in Korea the service is especially attentive. Beauty parlours provide women with similar services as barbershops.

Barbershops (*ibalso*) abound throughout Seoul and other Korean cities and towns, and most large hotels provide luxurious versions of this traditional service. The initial haircut or perfunctory trim only takes about ten minutes, after which 'the works' commence. While one attendant gives you a thorough manicure, another strops a razor for a shave, which in Korea usually includes the fringes of forehead, eyebrows, nose, ears and neck.

Next comes a stimulating head and body massage. These massages (*an-ma*, or 'press-and-rub') often include special acupressure performed by trained specialists in that ancient Oriental therapy.

Meanwhile, someone else probes your inner ear with a long instrument to scrape out excess wax and accumulated dirt. After scraping, the canal is cleaned and lubricated with a small wad of cotton on a stick. People claim that hearing is greatly enhanced after a Korean ear cleansing.

Other barbershop treatments include hot towels, facial creams, pedicures, and complimentary cigarettes and tea. After you have been thoroughly trimmed, shaved, scraped, creamed and massaged, a towel is gently placed over your eyes to lull you into a short nap. By the time you float out of a Korean barbershop an hour or two later, you will feel and look like a new person, all for US$10−15, depending on the location and luxury of the place.

Bathhouses (*mogyok-tang*) are another traditional form of relaxation in Korea. Koreans are fanatics about bathing and personal hygiene, and there are public bathhouses for both men and women throughout the country. Public bathhouses are identified by this symbol:

As in Japan, you are expected to soap, scrub and rinse yourself thoroughly outside of the big tubs and communal pools prior to stepping in. Faucets with wash basins and showers are provided for this purpose. After you are clean, it is time for a leisurely, soothing soak in the communal pool, which is usually kept very hot. After that, repeat the cycle with another good scrubbing and soaking.

In addition to the main communal pool and washing facilities, most public bathhouses have extra-hot and extra-cold tubs for those who wish to give their pores a stimulating work-out. Some bathhouses also have saunas. For a nominal fee, you get a bar of soap, a small towel, and an abrasive washcloth on the premises. Koreans dry off by rubbing themselves repeatedly with what Westerners spurn as mere 'hand-towels', wringing out excess moisture after each rubbing. It works very well.

After washing, soaking, scrubbing and towelling themselves, most Koreans stretch out in a corner or in a separate lounging room for a snooze. Bathhouses remain open from 6 am until 9 pm so there is plenty of time for a nap. No one ever seems to be in a hurry to leave a bathhouse or barbershop in Korea.

For additional luxury in bathing (at additional cost), one might try what is called a *sauna-tang*. This is a fancier and more private version of the traditional public bathhouse, complete with your own individual berth on a heated *ondol*-floor, a small closet, pillow and sheets, a dressing gown, and a menu offering all sorts of food and drink. Expert masseurs provide bracing rub-downs between trips to the various hot and cold pools and sauna rooms. In addition to private napping areas, *sauna-tang* also provide a plush communal lounging room with reclining chairs, colour television and a snack counter.

One of the most popular *sauna-tang* in Seoul is located in the Shin Shin Hotel, an old establishment set in an alley next to the Bank of Korea's head office near the Shinsegye Department Store.

Down in the provinces, especially near mountain parks, the most popular places for bathing are the many natural hot spring spas located there. These are marvellous places to relax during runs along Korea's tourist trails.

In hotels and inns throughout the country, professional masseurs or masseuses — massage is the traditional occupation of the blind in the Far East — may be called to your room to 'press-and-rub' those knots and kinks from your muscles and joints.

this famous dish at the **Han Il Kwan Restaurant**, an old establishment with an excellent reputation throughout Korea.

While in Chonju, also stop to visit one of Korea's finest private antique shop/museums, the **Chon Bok Tuk San Pun Chon**. Among the many superb antiques on display and for sale there are Silla ceramics, traditional Korean folk masks, antique jewellery, and much more.

Temples and Mountain Parks

From Chonju there are numerous interesting side-trips to ancient temples and scenic mountain parks. Take a bus or cab, or drive yourself, to the **Songgwang Temple**, en route to nearby Mt Mai. The walls and ceilings of this attractive temple are covered with some of the most colourful Buddhist murals in Korea.

From Songgwang-sa continue onward towards **Mt Mai**, Horse Ears Mountain, which takes its name from two peaks which look like horse ears when viewed from the northern approach at Chinan village. Hike up to **Hwaom** Cave through the Chonghwang Pass, then continue along the trail until you reach one of Korea's most unusual religious sites, the **T'Ap-sa**, or Pagoda Temple. An eccentric hermit named Yi Kap-yong spent a lifetime here piling up thousands of unmortared stones to form dozens of crude 'Shaking Pagodas', ranging from a few centimetres to nine metres (30 feet) in height. Incredibly, most of them have survived centuries of weather and warfare. T'ap-sa is not a Buddhist temple, but rather a shrine to the hermit Yi's own personal form of religion, probably an obscure sect of animism. The paths beyond the Shaking Pagodas lead to several more orthodox temples nearby.

Thirty-two kilometres (20 miles) southwest of Chonju, surrounded by the wooded slopes of Mt Moak, sits the **Kumsan** (Gold Mountain) **Temple**. Founded in AD 599 and further enlarged in 766, the entire complex was destroyed by the Japanese in 1592. It was rebuilt again during the mid-17th century.

The three-storey Miruk-Jon, or main hall, makes Kumsan-sa the tallest temple in Korea. Inside stands an 11-metre (36-foot) gilt statue of Maitreya Buddha. Outside stands a superb six-tiered Paekche pagoda. In the second hall sits a large Buddha surrounded by sculptures of 500 disciples.

From Chonju or the Kumsan Temple, return to the Honam (Seoul-Sunchon) Expressway and proceed south to **Mount Naejan** (Inner Sanctum) **National Park**, one of Korea's favourite destinations for autumn scenery. The colonnaded approach of red maple bears testimony to this favoured spot. The primary cultural attraction here is **Paegyang** (White Sheep) **Temple** founded in AD 632. It was destroyed

four times and finally rebuilt for a fifth time in 1917 by the Zen master Sangmanam. A tourist hotel provides comfortable lodging for those wishing to spend an extra day wandering through this lovely mountain park. In October, when many of the mountain parks close to Seoul are crowded, Mt Naejan is a good choice for those wishing for a quieter atmosphere.

Kwangju: Food, Wine and Tea

Kwangju lies an hour's drive south of the Paegyang Temple. En route, bamboo lovers may wish to stop at **Tamyang**, Korea's bamboo craft capital, where mats, baskets, chopsticks, spoons and other useful items are fashioned from bamboo.

The final stop before the west side melts into the southern coast is **Kwangju**, capital of South Cholla Province. Like Chonju, Kwangju is famous for food, and a connoisseur would be hard pressed to decide which place offers superior fare. The fertile Honam agricultural basin provides the abundant and varied ingredients required to continue a great gourmet tradition started there many centuries ago by the region's discriminating noblemen. Kwangju also produces some of the best Korean liquors, most notably *chungchong* (barley and rice wine) and *makkolli* (fermented rice wine).

Kwangju is also famous for tea, especially the 'early spring tea' cultivated there by monks in the nearby mountains. The tender green leaves used for this delicious brew are hand-picked high in the mountains at just the right stage, then meticulously steamed and dried nine times in a long, tedious process which only monks seem to have the time and patience to perform. The resulting product is an exquisitely fragrant tea which is said to purify the blood, refresh the spirit, improve appetite and promote digestion.

At the foot of **Mudung Mountain**, which stands guard over the city, is a new resort area with comfortable accommodation. At the **Kwangju Museum** are fascinating exhibits of porcelain and other relics recovered from a Chinese ship which sunk in the Yellow Sea off the Korean coast 600 years ago.

Kwangju is a convenient launching point for tours of the southern coast. For an abbreviated southern tour, proceed east along the expressway from Kwangju directly to Sunchon and head for Pusan, stopping off along the way to visit various mountains, temples and coastal resorts. For the complete southern swing, travel south from Kwangju to Mokpo, a port town perched on the extreme southwestern tip of the peninsula. From there work your way along the coastline to Sunchon and onward to points beyond.

The Scenic Southern Seaboard

The southern seaboard is the site of Korea's most beautiful national sea park, the Hallyo Waterway. Stretching from Chungmu and Hansan Island across to Yosu and Namhae, the Hallyo Waterway is dotted with 115 inhabited and 253 uninhabited islands. These islands protect the Hallyo Waterway from the rougher seas of the Straits of Korea to the south. A region of unparalleled coastal beauty, the Hallyo Waterway was declared a National Park in 1968.

By car from Pusan, the quickest way to get to the Hallyo Waterway is to follow the Pusan-Sunchon Expressway to Masan, then take Route 2 south to Chungmu, which is the most popular destination in the Hallyo Waterway. Otherwise, the most comfortable and scenic route is by hydrofoil, which runs four times a day between Pusan and Chungmu, and takes 1.5 hours. Hydrofoils also connect Pusan and Yosu, as well as other points in the Hallyo Waterway.

If you come from the west side of Korea, start your southern excursion in Kwangju, and follow the routes in reverse.

The Hallyo Waterway

The rustic coastal town of **Chungmu**, which remains virtually untouched by modern development, is the most convenient spring-board for tours of the Hallyo Waterway. From there one can cover all other points of interest.

The hydrofoil from Pusan will stop at Changsungpo, a tiny town on Koje Island. From there you may hire private launches to take you to **Haekumgang**, an impressive outcropping of sheer cliffs which rise straight out of the blue waters on the southern shores of the island. Covered with pine and camellia, this rocky bluff is one of Hallyo's six designated scenic wonders. It is also a refuge for egrets and seabirds from southern Pacific waters. Excursion boats also run out to Haekumgang directly from Chungmu.

Chungmu is a delightful little town which gives excellent impressions of traditional Korean coastal life. Few buildings stand over two storeys high, and what little evidence there is of the 20th century is all of 1950s vintage. An interesting open market starts at the pier and sprawls for blocks. From the pier, ferries take tourists out for sightseeing on nearby scenic islands, and excursion boats carry sportsmen out to fish, scuba-dive, sail and water-ski. There are many good Korean inns in town, but the best place to stay is the **Chungmu Tourist Hotel**, located across the bridge from town on Miruk Island.

Besides its lovely seascapes, Chungmu has a few cultural attractions. Near the Chungmu Tourist Hotel is the **Yong-hwa Temple**,

founded by a Zen monk in AD 632. Destroyed and rebuilt twice, Yong-hwa-sa today is a public temple as well as a functioning monastery and hermitage. Here you may observe robed monks going about their daily monastic chores as they have for 1,600 years.

On a hill overlooking downtown Chungmu stands the impressive **Sebyonggwan Hall**, built in 1603 to commemorate Korea's victory over Japan in the Imjin War of 1592–8. At one time 548 gunboats and 36,009 sailors were stationed here. The ceiling and beam decor are particularly fine, and inside is a series of old paintings done on wood panels, depicting Admiral Yi's heroic battles.

Chungmu and the entire Hallyo Waterway are associated with the naval victories of Admiral Yi, Korea's greatest hero, and memorials to him are everywhere to be seen here. Indeed, the name 'Chungmu' is derived from Admiral Yi's posthumous honourific title: 'Chung' or 'Loyalty' and 'Mu' or 'Martial Valour'. His greatest victory occurred in the shallow waters off Hansan Island, when his paltry fleet of 12 armour-clad Turtle Ships drove directly into an armada of 133 Japanese warships and won.

A scenic two-hour excursion takes you from the pier at Chungmu out to **Hansan Island**, and includes an hour to stroll around the island. Walk around the quiet cove to the **Chesungdang Shrine**, an elaborate complex of classical pavilions founded by Admiral Yi for use as his naval headquarters during the Imjin War. Every structure has been beautifully renovated in authentic Yi Dynasty style, and the entire island-park is meticulously landscaped.

A ferry ride west from Chungmu will bring you to **Samchonpo**, a protected area for the preservation of Korea's dwindling egrets, now designated as 'living national treasures'. One can see them congregrate — a mass of snow-white feathers, long legs, and sharp fishing bills — on nearby Hakdo islet, where they nest in the tops of old pine trees.

Both local ferries and the Pusan hydrofoils run across to **Yosu**, the western terminus of the Hallyo Waterway. Yosu has a small tourist hotel and is known as an excellent fishing area. Excursion boats may be hired for fishing or sightseeing. Shuttles run from Yosu to nearby **Odong Island**, which is covered with colourful camellia and is famous for a special breed of bamboo which Admiral Yi used to fashion arrows for his troops. Another shuttle connects Yosu to **Namhae**, the second largest island in the waterway after Koje. A 660-metre (2,050-foot) long suspension bridge — the longest in the Orient — connects this island to the mainland.

Historic Chinju

From Yosu, Samchonpo and Namhae, buses run regularly up to
Chinju, a quintessentially Korean town seldom visited by foreigners. If
you are driving from Chungmu, return to Masan along Route 2, then
take the Pusan-Sunchon Expressway west to Chinju.

Recently renovated **Chinju Castle** was the site of two historic
battles during the Imjin War. During the first battle, Japanese invaders
were repulsed after prolonged and fierce fighting. A year later, the
Japanese attacked again, and after an equally bloody battle, Korean
forces were defeated and Chinju was overrun. To celebrate their
victory, Japanese officers held a big banquet at Choksongnu Pavilion
in Chinju Castle. Among the Korean *kisaeng* brought in to entertain
the Japanese commanders was Chu Non-gae, a highly accomplished
kisaeng whose patron, a Korean officer, had been killed in the defence
of Chinju. During the party, Chu Non-gae plied an important Japanese
general with wine, then enticed him out for a romantic stroll in the
moonlight along a scenic cliff overlooking the Nam River. At the edge
of a steep precipice, she threw her arms passionately around the
general, manoeuvered him to the brink, then leapt into the river,
dragging him down with her to their death. Her patriotic sacrifice is
celebrated every year with a ceremony at a shrine built in her honour
above the rock.

Mount Chiri National Park

From Chinju, follow the expressway about 80 kilometres (50 miles)
southwest to Hadong, then veer northwest for another 60 kilometres
(37 miles) until you reach the town of Kurye, which sits at the southern
edge of **Mt Chiri National Park**.

Approaching Mt Chiri from Kurye, one comes across the **Hwaom
Temple**, located in a scenic mountain valley. Founded in the sixth
century, it was expanded by the great Buddhist priest Uisang in 643
and houses several national treasures, including a five-metre (16.5-
foot) stone lantern — the largest of its kind in Korea — from the Silla
Dynasty.

Further into the foothills stands the **Sanggye Temple**, founded in
723 by a monk returning from a pilgrimage to China. It is said that
when he visited China, he bribed a temple attendant at the Kaiyum
Temple to give him the skull of the revered Zen patriarch Hui-Neng.
Returning to Korea with his ill-gotten relic, he erected a shrine in Mt
Chiri to house his prize, and this later became the Sanggye Temple.

Further north, on the western edge of Mt Chiri National Park, lies
the ancient town of **Namwon**, where there is a beautiful little inn with

a classical Japanese garden, which used to serve as a hunting lodge during Japan's occupation of Korea. Namwon was immortalized in Korean history by the romantic tale of Chunhyang and Myong-nyong, a true story which has formed the theme of countless Korean movies, books, and plays.

Myong-nyong, the son of an aristocrat, fell in love with Chunhyang, the daughter of a *kisaeng*. Their romance blossomed, and they married in secret, for their parents would never condone such a match in Korea's ultra-conservative Confucian society. Soon thereafter, Myong-nyong's father was transferred to a post in the capital, and the young lovers were separated. A corrupt and licentious governor was at that time posted at Namwon, and he resolved to add the beautiful Chunhyang to his list of conquests. She adamantly refused to comply with his persistent demands, and the enraged governor had her kidnapped, imprisoned and mercilessly beaten under his personal supervision. About that time, Myong-nyong was appointed Royal Inspector for Cholla Province. Hearing of Chunhyang's plight, he rushed to her rescue and severely punished the offending governor. Bride and groom then returned to Seoul together, where they lived happily ever after. Chunhyang's fidelity, a hallowed Confucian virtue, is celebrated annually on the eighth day of the fourth lunar month (around mid-March) at a shrine in Namwon erected in her honour.

Songgwang Temple

From Mt Chiri Park return to Kurye and proceed due south about 40 kilometres (25 miles) to Sunchon. From Sunchon there is regular bus service up to the Songgwang Temple, one of Korea's three largest temples and the centre of the Son (Zen) sect. The one-hour ride is scenic all the way. If you are visiting this temple directly from Pusan, the express bus to Sunchon takes four hours. If you come down from Kwangju, Sunchon is only an hour by express bus.

Songgwang Temple was originally founded as a hermitage during the Silla era, but it was expanded into a full-scale temple during the 12th century by Pojo, the great Zen master, and his disciples. It boasts many exquisite examples of traditional Korean temple architecture from different historical periods. For example, the two covered bridges which cross the small stream at the temple's entrance are unique architectural features seldom seen elsewhere.

Today, Songgwang Temple is most renowned for its small but permanent retinue of resident foreign monks and nuns. It is the only temple in Korea with arrangements for transmitting the *dharma* to Western novices. On entering the order, fledgling monks and nuns must first spend three to six months doing kitchen duty and maintenance work. If after that their resolve has not weakened, they embark on a strict regimen of intense meditation, with regular stints of farmwork in between. Most of the foreigners speak little or no Korean, yet they still manage to progress in their studies and live in harmony with Korean monks and nuns. Currently Songgwang houses four monks from America, three from Canada, two from England, two from Taiwan, one from Japan, one from Sri Lanka and one from France. Visitors may stay overnight in very traditional quarters provided by the temple, which also serves delicious meals of Buddhist vegetarian cuisine. Those interested in the application of Buddhism to the Western world should make a point to visit this remote Zen temple when touring the southern coast.

Cheju-Do: 'Over There'

Located 90 kilometres (56 miles) off the southern coast of the peninsula, Cheju is Korea's largest island and the only island province in the republic. This egg-shaped isle is 71 kilometres (44 miles) long and 41 kilometres (25 miles) wide, with a population of about half a million people. Entirely volcanic in composition, the island is dominated by the 1,950-metre (6440-foot) lava cone of **Mt Halla**, the highest peak in Korea.

Cheju is distinctly different from mainstream Korea. The island's shamanist roots are still very evident, with stone altars for performing *kut* (shaman ceremonies) maintained in almost every village, and phallic fertility symbols scattered everywhere. Shaman mediums, mostly women, perform ceremonial seances to exorcise homes of evil spirits, invoke the gods of fertility, or contact the souls of departed spirits. Cheju is exotic.

The popularity of shamanism in Cheju is related to another distinctive feature of the island. Since it is traditionally a matriarchal society, it is common for men in Cheju to stay home and take care of the house and children while women go out and earn the family's bread. In fact, one of Cheju's most popular attractions are the *haenya* (women divers), living legends who still ply their age-old trade along the island's rocky shores. Ranging in age from 10 to 60, these hardy women plunge to depths of 12−18 metres (40−60 feet) and stay under for three to five minutes without the aid of breathing equipment. Much of the excellent seafood served in Cheju's restaurants is hauled from the sea floors by the *haenya*. These aggressive, independent women exert a special fascination for Japanese and Korean men, who are accustomed to docile women.

Even Cheju's economy is different. With its relatively mild, almost sub-tropical climate, the island has become Korea's citrus centre, producing oranges, tangerines, grapefruits and pineapples for both domestic consumption and export markets. The 'Cheju orange', a hybrid of local and imported species, has become a state-of-the-art fruit in the Far East. Cheju's most distinctive crop is rape (mustard seed) — its bright yellow blossoms paint endless acres of farmland with golden hues and have become one of the island's hallmarks.

Cheju has a colourful history. Until about AD 1000, the island remained aloof and uninfluenced by events in mainland Korea. During the Koryo Dynasty, it finally received the Korean name 'Cheju', which simply means 'over there'. For centuries, the Korean court used Cheju as an island of exile, banishing disgraced officials and criminals to its remote shores. As a result, most Koreans once regarded Cheju with a mixture of fear and disdain.

During the 13th century, Cheju was overrun by the Mongols, who used the island as a staging ground for their abortive attempts to conquer Japan. The local dialect is derived directly from Mongolian, and in the more remote mountain villages Mongol-style clothing and implements are still in use.

Cheju was the first place in Korea visited by Westerners, albeit accidentally. On 16 August 1653, the Dutch ship *Sparrow Hawk*, en route from the Dutch enclave in Taiwan to Nagasaki in Japan, encountered a severe typhoon in the Straits of Korea and was wrecked on the shores of Cheju. The surviving Dutch crew were detained there for 13 years. After their escape to Japan and return to Europe, one of them, Henrik Hammel, wrote a lengthy account of their capitivity in Korea and his book, *The Dutch Come to Korea*, became the first account of the Hermit Kingdom to be published in the West.

Cheju continued its peripheral role in Korea until the mid-1960s, when President Park visited the island and took a personal interest in its development. Since then, Cheju has grown at a rapid pace, and today it is one of Korea's major resort centres.

Cheju City and the Northern Shore

The main town is Cheju City, located midway along the northern shore. Although Cheju City retains a small town atmosphere and consists mostly of two-floor storefronts, with few high-rises to mar the skylines, it is also a tourist town, with its own airport, several deluxe hotels, numerous local inns, restaurants, nightclubs and shops.

On the northwestern outskirts of town is one of the island's most popular sights, the **Yong Du** (Dragon Head) **Rock**. This outcropping of basalt was formed when molten lava from Mt Halla flowed into the sea and abruptly hardened. However, legend tells a different story: according to this, the Dragon King sent a messenger to Mt Halla to obtain the secret 'Elixir of Immortality' from the Mountain God. Angered by this rude intrusion, the Mountain God shot the messenger with an arrow, petrifying him as a rock by the sea.

Sobudu (West Pier) is a popular place to stroll in Cheju City and provides interesting glimpses into the life-styles of local fishing families. Ten minutes' drive east of town is the **Cheju Folklore Museum**, which has a modest but interesting collection of local artefacts.

Along the northern shore are five good swimming beaches. **Samyong Beach**, a ten-minute drive east of town, and **Hamdok Beach**, another 15-minute drive further east, are the most popular and have adequate facilities for food and lodging. Kimnyong, Sehwari and

Kwakji are smaller, less crowded beaches.

Halfway between Cheju City and Hallim lies **Hanpaduri**, the remains of a fortress which has been dedicated as a memorial to Korea's patriotic 'Sambyolcho' troops, who refused to capitulate to Mongol sovereignty when the Koryo Dynasty surrendered. For years they bravely defended the honour of Koryo from their bastion on Cheju — much as Ming loyalists resisted Manchu rule for decades from Taiwan — but they were finally vanquished by overwhelming Mongol forces.

On the northeastern corner of the island is the famous **Manjang Snake Cave**, whose 71-kilometre (44-mile) length makes it the longest known lava tunnel in the world. Varying in diameter from three to 20 metres (ten to 80 feet), the interior is lit with floodlamps and may be explored by tourists. Prior to 1625, a virgin girl was sacrificed at the entrance to this cave every year in order to appease the Snake God. This shaman practice was ended when a new magistrate arrived from the Korean court and introduced the more civilized Buddhist practice of supplicating spirits with ritual offerings of food and wine.

Sogwipo and the Southern Shore

On the southern shore of the island, directly opposite Cheju City, lies the little town of **Sogwipo**, famous for its beaches, waterfalls and oranges. You can get there quickly from Cheju City by taking either of two cross-island highways which skirt around the base of Mt Halla, or more slowly by taking the round-the-island road.

A few minutes' drive east of Sogwipo is beautiful **Chong-bang Waterfall**, a 22-metre (75-foot) cascade of water which is said to be the only waterfall in Asia which drops directly into the sea. To the west of town is another famous waterfall, called **Chonji-yon**.

Sogwipo is Korea's citrus capital, producing oranges, grapefruits and tangerines in great abundance. Protective walls of lava rock have been built up around the orchards to protect them from the island's constant winds. In addition to growing citrus, this little town prepares superb seafood, which is served at small seaside eateries along the coast.

Thirty minutes' drive west of Sogwipo lies **Chungmun Beach**, one of Cheju's finest swimming resorts. Nearby is **Chunju-yon Waterfall**, with a clear, cool pool so alluring that legend says it once served as the bathing pool of the gods.

An extensive resort complex is planned for Chungmun Beach. It will ultimately include ten tourist hotels, six Korean inns, three motels, 130 private villas and three shopping centres, plus restaurants, bars, cafés, a marina for boating and fishing, and other recreational

facilities. It is hoped that these will be developed with the same good taste and judgement evident in Korea's mainland tourist resorts, such as Kyongju and the national mountain parks.

The West Shore

On the west shore are Hyopjae Beach and the nearby Hyopjaegul Cave, another well known lava tunnel. But the biggest attraction on the west side is the **Hallim Handweavers Complex**, located in the coastal village of Hallim.

Established twenty years ago by Father Patrick J McGlinchey, a Catholic priest who has resided in Korea for nearly 40 years, the Hallim Handweavers produce some of the best Irish woollens outside of Ireland. The equipment as well as the sheep were brought to Cheju by Father McGlinchey during the early 1960s, and all work — from shearing, washing, carding and spinning to warping, threading, steaming and weaving — is done by hand. Only traditional Irish patterns are woven, and the superb sweaters, scarves, caps, mittens, blankets and piece goods produced here may be purchased at the weaving complex in Hallim, or at their exclusive store in the shopping arcade of the Chosun Hotel in Seoul. Prices, which are the same in Seoul as in Cheju, are quite reasonable for such high-quality handwork, and the annual demand for Hallim's woollen products consistently exceeds the supply.

Father McGlinchey is also founder and president of the 'Isidore Development Association', a non-profit organization which engages in various social projects around the island. The handweaving cottage industry is one of there. You may visit the Isidore Ranch, a 20-minute drive into the hills from Hallim, for a look at the furry flocks and a chat with the good father.

Sunrise Peak and Other Sights

Il-Chul-Bong (Sunrise Peak) is located at Songsanpo, a tiny village on the extreme eastern edge of the island. The site is so beautiful that you may want to spend a night or two at the nearby Sunrise Hotel.

The summit, famous for beautiful sunrises, is part of the Seonsan Promontory, which boasts 99 exotically shaped lava peaks. A sheer cliff of lava rock pocked with caves, Sunrise Peak provides the most panoramic vistas on the island. As you reach the summit, the dark crater of this ancient volcanic cone yawns up at you. Beyond lies the offshore island of Udo and the shimmering waters of the Straits of Korea.

Among Cheju's best-known sights are the 52 **Tol-Harubang** (Grandfather Stones) which stand scattered around the island. These are phallic statues of humans which bear oddly bemused expressions; these images remain Cheju's greatest mystery, for no one knows when they were sculpted or to what purpose. They bear an uncanny resemblance to the primitive stone statuary found scattered around Tahiti, Okinawa, Fiji and Easter Island. You can view some excellent specimens in front of Cheju City's **Samsonghyol Museum** or **Kwandok-jok Pavilion**, a 15th-century structure which is the oldest building on Cheju.

Mt Halla itself is one of the island's most popular sightseeing attractions, and a cross-island highway passes on either side of the summit. On the southwestern slope, about three kilometres (two miles) from the top, is **Yongsil**, a jumble of jagged crags, bizarre stone formations and other strange shapes created by petrified lava. Halfway between Mt Halla and the east coast lies a very old village called **Chongup**, where ancient customs handed down from the island's original inhabitants persist.

Accommodation

There are numerous hotels and inns around Cheju Island, and more are opening every year. In Cheju City, your best bet is probably the elegant **Cheju Grand Hotel**: new, deluxe and tastefully appointed with Oriental furnishings and fixtures.

More centrally located in Cheju City is the **KAL Hotel**, which has smaller rooms and somewhat lower rates than the Grand. The hotel's biggest attraction is a large casino, but during the peak seasons of April-May and August-October the hotel is usually crowded with tour groups from Japan.

A little east of Sogwipo is Cheju's famous **Honeymoon House**, a single-storey hotel which caters primarily, but not exclusively, to newlyweds. Set serenely among quiet gardens and shaded groves high on a hillside overlooking the sea, the Honeymoon House is popular among couples in search of romantic atmosphere and privacy.

Another good place to stay is the **Sunrise Hotel** at the foot of Sunrise Peak on the east coast. Here, because of its location, you stand a relatively good chance of dragging yourself out of bed in time to hike up to the peak and see a glorious sunrise.

In addition to the tourist hotels, Cheju has numerous local inns, where both the accommodation and the prices are far more modest than at the deluxe places.

Getting to Cheju

From Seoul, Korean Airlines operates 106 flights per week to Cheju, with a flight-time of 55 minutes. The 40-minute flight from Pusan operates 53 times a week, and the 50-minute flight from Taegu takes off 14 times a week. From Kwangju, KAL flights operate 14 times a week to Cheju, and from Yosu they depart seven times a week, with a flight-time of 40 minutes.

The leisurely, scenic way to travel to Cheju is by boat. A car-ferry operates daily between Pusan and Cheju and takes 11.5 hours. This is the most convenient way to go if you are seeing Korea by car. Regular passenger ferries run daily to Cheju from Mokpo in six hours, and every other day from Yosu in four hours.

Off The Beaten Track

Andong and Hahoe

For a look at the courtly life-styles lived by Korea's Confucian scholar-gentry during the Yi Dynasty, take a side-trip to Andong and Hahoe. The most convenient approach is due west along Route 34 from the eastern coastal town of Yongdok, a drive that takes about one hour. The rather roundabout train route from Seoul requires about six hours.

Andong is the ancestral home of the Kwon clan, an important *yangban* (aristocrat) family which held many high government posts during the Yi Dynasty. In Andong one still sees wizened old *yangban* gentlemen in traditional *hanbok* outfits, complete with broad-brimmed horse-hair hats covering their top-knots, stroking their long wispy whiskers while smoking and chatting under shade trees. Several large, old gentry dwellings have survived in Andong, and they give excellent impressions of classical Korean residential architecture, as well as reflections of traditional *yangban* life-styles. In town one also finds the Buddhist **Taewon Temple** next to the **Songdang Church**, a classical Catholic church of red brick.

Twenty-eight kilometres (17 miles) north of Andong is the **Tosan Sowon Confucian Academy**, a typical institute of higher learning in the classical Confucian tradition. It was founded by Yi Whang, Korea's foremost Confucian scholar, during the late 16th century. Though no longer actively used, the ancient structures as well as numerous Confucian academic artefacts are well preserved here. If you take the bus from Andong up to Tosan Sowan, you will have to walk the last two kilometres (1.2 kilometres) from the bus-stop along a paved road. By private car you may drive right up to the gate.

Even more remote than Andong is the little hamlet of **Hahoe**, a half-hour drive southwest from Andong. The last eight kilometres (five miles) is a slow winding drive along unpaved roads. In Hahoe, little has changed during the past 500 years, especially the architecture. Note the ancient architectural styles here, from the simple thatch huts of farmers to the spacious elegant villas of *yangban* families. The only evidence of the 20th century in this charming old village is the occasional TV antenna jutting up from ancient eaves and electric wires running along weathered wooden beams.

Pusok Temple

Pusok-sa (Floating Rock Temple) is one of Korea's most inaccessible temples. It is so remote that Japanese troops never found it during their destructive rampage through Korea in 1592−8. Consequently, Pusok-sa preserves some of the country's most ancient temple structures and authentic Buddhist artefacts. The temple lies about 60 kilometres (37 miles) due north of Andong along Route 5. It is a long, bumpy ride along dusty, unpaved roads, but for intrepid travellers and devoted students of Buddhist culture, the effort to reach this distant temple will prove richly rewarding.

The temple was established in AD 676 by the great Silla priest Uisang, after his return from China. During his youth, Uisang fell in love with a beautiful girl named Myohwa (Delicate Flower). So lovely and delicate was she that before Uisang could marry her, she was whisked away to the capital by court officials and sent as a gift to the emperor of Tang China. Heart-broken and inconsolable, Uisang entered the priesthood and ultimately became one of Korea's greatest holy men. During his pilgrimage to China, he crossed paths with his old love Myohwa, whose devotion to him was so strong that her spirit followed his boat back to Korea and transformed itself into an enormous boulder that protected him and his new temple from the thieves which infested the area. This 'floating rock' still hangs precariously outside the temple's main hall.

According to the story, Myohwa later took the form of a stone dragon and burrowed beneath the temple, with her head at the altar and her tail 18 metres (60 feet) away by the lantern. Interestingly, several years ago a team of professors from Donggju University came down from Seoul to study Pusok-sa scientifically. They excavated an area near the lantern in front of the main hall and soon uncovered part of a large stone formation shaped exactly like a dragon's tail. They were even more astounded to find scales clearly etched onto the stone. Unwilling to disturb the sleeping dragon and unable to offer a 'scientific' explanation for their find, they abandoned the project and returned to Seoul.

Ullung Island

This is one of Korea's least known, least visited and most interesting destinations. It lies 268 kilometres (166 miles) northeast of Pohang, halfway between Korea and Japan. You can get there in six hours from Pohang by taking the *Han Il Ho* express boat, which drops you off in **To-dong**, the island's main town, located on the southeast coast.

To-dong has a refreshing air of rustic island charm, with simple functional dwellings and few modern structures. There are many good *yogwan* in town, and those located along Todong Harbour provide superb views of the sea and fishing boats. Many doors in Ullung have

(Left) Olympic Stadium
during the Asian Games
spectacular.

(Top Right) Hodori, *the
Olympic teddy mascot*

*(Bottom Right) Three
track competitors at the
Asian Games.*

no locks: the island is known for its absolute absence of crime.

The island is ideal for leisurely hikes. Along a path behind Todong you can find a famous natural mineral spring whose waters spurt from a sculpted stone tortoise head. **Songinbong**, at 984 metres (3250 feet) Ullung's highest peak, requires about half a day to hike up and back. Only recently has a paved road around the entire island been completed; cars can be hired in Todong for round-the-island tours.

Another pleasant way to see Ullung is by boat. Hire a launch at Todong Harbour to take you around the island, stopping here and there at scenic spots and nearby islets. Ullung's beaches feature especially clear blue water, the best being at **Watari** on the east coast. This beach has a sparkling waterfall that cascades into a salt-water pool by the sea. On the southwest shore is **Satekam Beach**, a serene swimming retreat set in a quiet cove with warm unruffled waters.

Boating off the northeast coast, one comes across a dense patch of aquatic rock formations which jut up abruptly from the sea. A variety of sea-birds nest in this exotic stone grotto.

Off Ullung's east coast sits **Chuk Island**, an unusually productive little island easily reached by boat. A hard trek brings you up to the island's plateau where there is a cattle farm of pampered, corn-fed stock that produces Korea's most tasty and tender beef. New calves from the mainland are hauled up to the top on the backs of sturdy farmers, and fattened cattle are lowered by rope and pulley to barges down below.

Along the shores of Ullung, women divers plunge underwater to gather lobsters, crabs, prawns, abalone and other delectable 'fruits of the sea', much as the women of Cheju do. The men fish for squid at night, but under far more comfortable conditions. Stringing bright lights from their boats to attract the fish, they bob along the dark waters, dry and cosy as they fish. Visitors may arrange to join these fishing excursions by enquiring at the harbour.

Sports

Koreans have a keen interest in sports and are formidable athletic competitors. They have participated in the Olympics since 1946, winning their first Gold Medal, in the free-style wrestling event, in the 1976 Montreal Olympics. They host the Olympics in 1988. In the 1986 Asia Games, Korea wrested second place from the Japanese and came within two medals of displacing the victorious Chinese team.

Visitors to Korea will find ample opportunity to keep in shape by participating in popular international sports, including the following described below.

Martial Arts

Taekwondo (the 'way of feet and fists') has been practised in Korea since 37 BC, or even earlier. It is a highly explosive fighting art in which the adept concentrates all mental and physical energy behind each blow and focusses the blow on specific vulnerable spots on his opponent's body. Different from both Chinese *kung fu* and Japanese *karate*, *taekwondo* is an indigenous Korean form of martial arts which has recently gained world-wide recognition as an international sporting event. In the 1979 Taekwondo Championships held in Germany, Koreans won the titles in seven out of ten divisions against athletes from 64 nations. The World Taekwondo Federation has its head-quarters at Kukki-won in the southern suburbs of Seoul, where it stages regular exhibitions of this ancient fighting art. Call the WTF at 776-2347 or 777-6080/9 for further information.

Trekking and Mountain Climbing

With 70 percent of the country covered with rugged mountains, trekking and mountain climbing have become popular pastimes in Korea. (In September 1977, Korean climbers scaled the peak of Mt Everest, making Korea the eighth nation to conquer that lofty summit.) Today, with over a dozen national mountain parks spread across the peninsula, trekking is the most accessible sport to foreign visitors. Since none of Korea's peaks exceeds 2,000 metres (6,300 feet), trekkers need not contend with extreme high altitudes, nor do they require expensive and cumbersome mountaineering gear. Good hiking shoes, proper clothing, and a light back-pack or shoulder-bag with basic necessities are all one needs to enjoy trekking and mountaineering in Korea.

Fishing

Surrounded on three sides by open seas, Korea has naturally evolved a strong fishing tradition. It remains a highly popular pastime throughout the country, and anglers can be seen wielding their poles on the banks of rivers, lakes, and reservoirs, as well as along the seashores of Korea. Popular fishing areas include the coast near Inchon, the offshore islands near Mokpo, the Hallyo Waterway (especially Yosu and Namhae), the Pusan area, Ullung Island, and the northeast coast. Fishing equipment is sold at very reasonable prices in sporting goods shops throughout the country, or it may be rented at certain resorts.

Skiing

Skiing has been popular in Korea ever since the sport was introduced by a missionary during the 1920s, and today the government is developing some of Korea's mountains into ski resorts. The best ski resort in Korea today is the Dragon Valley (Yongpyong) Ski Resort, located just below Mt Sorak and Mt Odae National Parks. Snow machines have extended the skiing season here, which now lasts from December until March. Ski lifts, ski schools, ski shops and other sports facilities make Dragon Valley a well-rounded winter resort. Accommodation is available at the Dragon Valley Hotel, Hotel Ju Won, private bungalows and Korean inns, as well as a large youth hostel. Ski resorts are also slated for development at Mt Sorak National Park and other mountainous regions in Korea.

Archery

Archery is a traditional sport in Korea, and at one time it was a required skill for all noblemen. The Korean Archery Association organizes annual archery contests at various historical celebrations and folk festivals throughout Korea. In Seoul, archery competitions and exhibitions are frequently held at the Pavilion of the Yellow Cranes, which is located just above Sajik Park.

Golf and Tennis

These two popular Western sports have spread rapidly in Korea in recent years. There are currently over 20 golf clubs in the country, and though these are membership clubs, guests are welcome to play. Most of the golf courses are located near Seoul, with a few down south at popular resort areas. Enquire at any hotel or tourist office.

Some of Korea's international hotels and resorts provide private tennis courts for guests, and many more courts are available at various

The National Flag

Korea's national flag deserves special mention. Unlike other national flags, which symbolize political divisions or celebrate specific historical events, the flag of Korea reflects ancient philosophical principles which apply equally to all countries. The emblem promotes contemplation rather than competition, and its symbolism has universal applications.

The central symbol is a circle divided into two comma-shaped halves. The upper red portion represents the *yang* or male principle, and the lower blue portion represents the *Um* (*yin* in Chinese) or female principle. This *yin/yang* symbol is derived from the *I-Ching*, or *Book of Changes*, an ancient Chinese book of divination which pre-dates Confucius by almost 1,000 years. The *yin/yang* symbol reflects opposite forces, acknowledges the inherent dualism of the universe, and offers the classical Taoist solution to contradictions: balance and harmony. This idea of balance and harmony amid opposing forces makes Korea's emblem a particularly appropriate symbol in international affairs.

The four trigrams arrayed around the central circle are also derived from the mysterious *Book of Changes*. The three solid lines in the upper left corner represent Heaven, and the three broken lines opposite represent Earth. In the upper right corner is the trigram for water, opposed by the trigram for fire in the lower left. Heaven and Earth, fire and water, *yin* and *yang* — these symbolize the forces of the universe. Man has responsibility to balance these forces for optimum social harmony and human progress.

In addition to its profound philosophical meaning, the Korean flag points to the ancient origins of Korean culture. The *yin/yang* and trigram symbols are central to Taoism. The selection of these symbols for Korea's national flag reflects the depth of Korean history and sophistication of Korean thought. It reaches beyond partisan politics to embrace profound philosophical principles of universal validity.

clubs, civic organizations and public parks throughout the land. Korean women picked up several gold medals in tennis at both the 1974 and 1978 Asian Games.

Horseback Riding and Racing

Equestrians may ride along the Han River in Seoul by visiting the riding stable operated by the Sheraton Walker Hill Hotel. It is located at the back entrance to the Sheraton complex. Horseback riding is also available at a few resorts in the south.

The only race track in Korea is located in southeastern Seoul across the Songsu Street Bridge. Operated by the Korean Equestrian Association, Happy Park holds races three days a week — on Saturday, Sunday and Monday.

Swimming

Some of Seoul's international hotels provide swimming pools for the use of their guests during the swimming season, which runs from May through October. As a peninsula, Korea is naturally fringed with salt-water beaches, and some of the better ones lie less than two hours from Seoul along the west coast near Inchon.

Basic Korean Vocabulary

The romanization system used by the Korean Ministry of Education, which prevails in local publications, differs significantly from the internationally recognized McCune-Reischauer system, which is used by most foreign scholars. Both systems appear haphazardly in literature, brochures, maps, menus and road signs, giving rise to such discrepancies as Kyongju/Gyeongju, Chonju/Jeonju, Pulkoki/Bulgogi, and so forth. To further confuse things, hyphens and apostrophes are thrown in or deleted according to the whims of the writer.

Do not attempt to show the romanized Korean words or phrases listed below to Korean people in hopes of establishing communication. Instead, repeat the words and phrases out loud several times until your pronunciation strikes a familiar bell in Korean ears.

Provided below are some basic Korean words, phrases, and sentence patterns which should suffice to get you around in most parts of the country.

Numerals

1	*Il*	50	*O-sip*
2	*Fe*	60	*Yik-sip*
3	*Sam*	70	*Ch'il-sip*
4	*Sa*	80	*Pal-sip*
5	*O*	90	*Ku-sip*
6	*Yuk*	100	*Paek*
7	*Ch'il*	200	*Ee-paek*
8	*Pal*	300	*Sam-paek*
9	*Ku*	846	*Pal-paek-sa-sip-yuk*
10	*Sip*	1,000	*Ch'on*
11	*Sip-ee*	2,000	*Ee-ch'on*
20	*Ee-sip*	5,729	*O-ch'on-ch'il-paek-ee-sip-ku*
30	*Sam-sip*	10,000	*Man*
40	*Sa-sip*	20,000	*Ee-man*
		etc.	

Greetings and Common Courtesy

Good morning	
Good afternoon	*Annyong ha-simnikka*
Good evening	
Hello	*Yobo-seyo*
Goodbye	*Annyong-hi ke-seyo*
Yes	*Ye*
No	*Anio*
Excuse me	*Sille-hamnida*
Thank you	*Kamsa-hamnida*

You're welcome	*Ch'onman-eyo*
I am sorry	*Mian-hamnida*
See you again	*To mannap-sida*
What is your name?	*Irumi muo-simnika?*
My name is ...	*Na-ui irumun ... imnida*
Just a moment, please	*Cham-kkan man kitari-seyo*
I beg your pardon	*Tasi malsumhae chu-seyo*

Useful Phrases and Sentence Patterns

Where is ...?	*... odi iss-umnikka?*
What is that?	*Jogosun muo-simnikka?*
That is good (right)	*Cho sumnida*
That is bad (wrong)	*Nappumnida*
You are beautiful	*Tangsinun yepumnida*
I like you	*Tangsinul joa-hamnida*
Please bring me some ...	*... chom kata chu-seyo*
Do you have ...?	*... iss-umnikka?*
How much does it cost?	*Olma imnikka?*
It is too expensive	*Nomu ppisamnida*
Can you give a discount?	*Discountu-rul hal-su-iss-umnikka?*
Can you speak English?	*Yong-o halsu-iss-umnikka?*
How long does it take to get there?	*Olmana kollimnikka?*
Please stop here	*Sewo chu-seyo*
What is this place called?	*Yogi-nun odi imnikka?*
Never mind	*Kokjong maseyo*

Basic Food and Drink

Korean food	*Han chong sik*
Cold water	*Naeng su*
Beer	*Maekchu*
This is delicious	*Aju masi sumnida*
Please bring the bill	*Kesanso-rul chusip-siyo*
Restaurant	*Sik-tang*
Bar	*Sul-jip*
Tearoom	*Tabang*

Places

Department Store	*Paekhwa-chom*
Duty free shop	*Myonse-pum-chom*
Local market	*Sijang*
Airport	*Konghang*
Seoul train station	*Seoul-yok*
Entrance	*Ipku*
Exit	*Ch'ulku*
Restroom	*Hwajang-sil*

Bank	*Unhaeng*
Hotel	*Hotel*
Good Korean inn	*Cho-un yogwan*
Post office	*Uche-kuk*
Police	*Pach'ul-so*
Public telephone	*Kongchung-chonhwa*
Subway	*Chi-hach'ol*
Terminal	*Chongjom*
Southgate Market	*Namdae-mun sijang*
Eastgate Market	*Dongdae-mun sijang*
Sejong Cultural Centre	*Sejong munhwa-hoekwan*

Sample Sentences:
Where is the restroom? *Hwajang-sil odi iss-umnikka?*
Please bring me some beer. *Maekchu chom kata chu-seyo.*
Do you have coffee? *Kopi iss-umnikka?*

Hangul: The Korean Language and Alphabet

The Korean language is one of the country's most distinctive traits. A member of the ancient Ural-Altaic family, the language today resembles Hungarian, Finnish and Turkish, rather than Chinese or Japanese.

Until the 15th century, Korean was written entirely with Chinese characters. The complex ideograms, which do not rely on phonetics, were borrowed intact from China and given Korean pronunciations. Consequently only the elite became literate.

All that changed with the invention of *hangul* (The Great Writing) during the reign of King Sejong. In 1443, he introduced his new writing system to the Korean court, stressing the national need for a convenient method for common people to express their thoughts and feelings in writing. *Hangul* could be quickly learned and easily used by all classes of people, and today it has given Korea one of the highest literacy rates in the world.

Hangul is the only alphabet in the world developed to fit the specific linguistic needs of a spoken language. Each letter was designed to resemble the shape taken by the lips, tongue and/or throat when producing the sound indicated. For example, the sound *n* is written ∟, representing the shape of the tongue pressing against the upper gum-ridge.

To be sure, Chinese ideograms are still used in combination with *hangul*, but they play a subordinate role and are used primarily for surnames, place names and other proper names. The entire Korean language can now be written exclusively in *hangul* without the use of a single Chinese ideogram.

Useful Addresses

Airlines with Regular Flights to Korea (Seoul Offices)

Air France
Room 218, Chosun Hotel
tel. 752−1027

Cathay Pacific
Room 701, Kolon Bldg
45 Mugyo-dong, Chung-ku
tel. 779−0321

China Airlines
Room 211, Chosun Hotel
tel. 755−1523

Japan Airlines
Room 101, Paiknam Bldg
188−3, 1-ka, Ulchiro, Chung-ku
tel. 757−1711

Korean Air
KAL Bldg
41−3 Sosomun-dong, Chung-ku
tel. 752−2221

KLM Royal Dutch Airlines
Room 110, Chosun Hotel
tel. 753−1093

Lufthansa German Airlines
Room 601, Centre Bldg
91−7 Sogong-dong, Chung-ku
tel. 777−9655

Malaysian Airlines
14th Fl, Dongbang Life Insurance Bldg
150, 2-ka, Taepyongno, Chung-ku
tel. 777−7761

Northwest Orient Airlines
Room 201, Chosun Hotel
tel. 753−6106

Saudi Arabian Airlines
Room 1301, Daeyeonkak Bldg
25−5, 1-ka, Chungmuro, Chung-ku
tel. 755−5621

Singapore Airlines
Room 202, Chosun Hotel
tel. 755−1226

Swiss Air
Room 301, Oriental Chemical Bldg
50, Sogong-dong, Chung-ku
tel. 757−8901

Thai Airways
Room 233, Chosun Hotel
tel. 779−2621

United Airlines
Room 512, New Korea Bldg
192−11, 1-ka, Ulchiro, Chung-ku
tel. 777−2993

Tourism Information Centres

The most efficient and helpful tourism organization in Korea is the Korea National Tourism Corporation (KNTC), which maintains Tourism Information Centres and a Tourist Complaint Centre in Seoul. They provide maps, brochures and useful information on tours, shopping, dining out and other activities. KNTC's Tourism Information Centre in Seoul is located at 10, Ta-dong, Chung-ku, tel. 757−0086. It is open every day from 9 am to 6 pm.

Suggestions and complaints may be registered by calling the Tourist Complaint Centre in Seoul at 735−0101.

Other Tourism Information Centres and their telephone numbers:
Seoul KNTC Main Centre: 757−0086; Kimpo Airport: 665−0086/0088; Seoul City Tourist Information Centre: 731−6337; Seoul Express Bus Terminal 598−3246: Chongro: 732−0088;

Kwanghwamun: 735—0088; Myong-dong: 757—0088; Namdaemun: 779—3644 and Tongdaemun: 272—0348.

Pusan Kimhae Airport: 98—1100; Railway Station: 463—4938 and Pukwan Ferry Terminal: 463—3161.

Cheju Cheju Airport: 42—0032.

Kyongju Railway Station: 2—3843; Pulguk Temple: 2—4747 and Express Bus Terminal: 2—9289.

KNTC's Major Overseas Offices

Frankfurt
Wiesenhutten Platz 26
6000 Frankfurt a.M.
Federal Republic of Germany
tel. 06—233226
tx. KNTCD 416127

Hong Kong
Rm. 506, Bank of America Bldg
12 Harcourt Rd
Hong Kong
tel. 5—238065
fax. 8450765

London
Vogue House, 2nd Floor
1, Hanover Square
London W1R 9RD, United Kingdom
tel. (01) 409—2100
tx. 266909 KNTCLDG

Los Angeles
510 West Sixth Street, Suite 323
Los Angeles, CA 90014
tel. (213) 623—1226/7
tx. KNTS LAXLSA 674935

New York, NY
Korea Centre Bldg.
460 Park Avenue, Suite 400
New York, NY 10022
tel. (212) 688—7543/4
tx. KNTCN YUR 225578

Paris
Tour Maine Montparnasse
33 Avenue de Maine, B.P. 169
75755 Paris Cedex 15 France
tel. 4538—7123
tx. KOTOUR 260825

Singapore
20—03 Clifford Centre
24 Raffles Places, Singapore 1
tel. 533—0441/2
tx. KOTOUR RS21673

Sydney
Suite 2101, Tower Bldg
Australia Sq, George St
Sydney 2000, Australia
tel. 27—4132/3
tx. KOTOUR AA23950

Taipei
Hsueh Chang Bldg, 6th Floor
259 Nanking E. Rd, Sec. 3
Taiwan
tel. 712—1264/5
tel. 25048 KNTCTPE

Tokyo
Room 124, Sanshing Bldg
4—1, 1-chome, Yuraku-Cho
Chiyoda-Ku, Tokyo, Japan
tel. (03) 580—3941, 508—2384
tx. J25377 KOTOUR

Embassies in Seoul

Argentina
135—53 Itaewon-dong
Yongsan-ku
tel. 793—4062

Australia
5—7 Fl, Salvation Army Bldg
58—1, 1-ka, Shinmunno
Chung-ku
tel. 730—6490

Austria
rm 1913, Kyobo Bldg
1−1, 1-ka, Chongno
Chung-ku
tel. 732−9071

Belgium
1−65 Tongbinggo-dong
Yongsan-ku
tel. 793−9611

Canada
10th Floor, Kolon Bldg
45 Mygyo-dong, Chung-ku
tel. 776−4062

Denmark
Suite 701, Namsong Bldg
260−199 Itaewon-dong, Yongsan-ku
tel. 795−4187

France
30 Hap-dong, Sodaemun-ku
tel. 362−5547

Germany
4th Floor, Daehan Fire & Marine
Insurance Bldg
51−1 Namchang-dong, Chung-ku
tel. 779−3272

India
37−3, Hannam-dong, Yongsan-ku
tel. 798−4257

Indonesia
55 Youido-dong, Yongdungpo-ku
tel. 782−5116

Italy
1−169, 2-ka, Shinmunno, Chongro-ku
736−5980

Japan
18−11 Chunghak-dong, Chongro-ku
tel. 733−5626

Malaysia
4−1 Hannam-dong, Yongsan-ku
tel. 795−9203

Mexico
901 Garden Tower Bldg
78−98 Unni-dong, Chongro-ku
tel. 741−4060

Netherlands
1−48, Tongbinggo-dong, Yongsan-ku
tel. 793−0651

New Zealand
Korean Publisher's Bldg
105−2 Sagan-dong, Chongro-ku
tel. 720−4255

Norway
124−12 Itaewon-dong, Yongsan-ku
tel. 792−6850

Philippines
559−510 Yoksam-dong
Kangnam-ku
tel. 568−9131

Republic of China (Taiwan)
83, 2-ka Myong-dong, Chung-ku
tel. 776−2721

Saudi Arabia
1−112, 2-ka, Shinmunno
Chongro-ku
tel. 739−0631

Spain
726−52 Hannam-dong, Yongsan-ku
tel. 794−3581

Sweden
8th Floor, Boyung Bldg
108−2 Pyong-dong, Chongro-ku
tel. 720−4767

Switzerland
32−10 Songwol-dong, Chongro-ku
tel. 739−9511

Thailand
653−7 Hannam-dong, Yongsan-ku
tel. 795−3098

United Kingdom
4 Chong-dong, Chung-ku
tel. 735−7341

USA
83 Sejongno, Chongro-ku
tel. 732−2601

Casinos in Korea

Seoul: Sheraton Walker Hill Hotel
tel. 453−0121

Pusan: Paradise Beach Hotel
tel. 277−2121

Inchon: Olympus Hotel
tel. 762−5181

Mt Sorak: Sorak Park Hotel
tel. 7−7711

Mt Songni: Songnisan Hotel
tel. 2091

Kyongju: Kolon Hotel
tel. 2−9001

Cheju: Cheju KAL Hotel
tel. 22−6151

Hyatt Regency Cheju Hotel
tel. 32−2001

Major International Banks in Seoul

Foreign

American Express International Banking Corp, tel. 23−2435/9
Bankers Trust Co, tel. 778−4411/9
Bank of America, tel. 778−4411/9
Chase Manhattan Bank, tel. 777−5781/94
Chemical Bank, tel. 776−9234/5
Citibank, tel. 28−4251/8
Marine Midland Bank, tel. 28−1580
First National Bank of Chicago,
tel. 23−9690/2
Barclays Bank International,
tel. 22−8573/6
Grindlays Bank Ltd, tel. 23−8411/5
Standard Chartered Bank, tel. 777−3191
Banque Nationale de Paris, tel. 23−2594/7
Credit Lyonnais, tel. 778−3811/5
The Bank of Tokyo, Ltd, tel. 777−6971/6
The Daiichi Kangyo Bank, Ltd,
tel. 777−9781/5
The Fuji Bank, Ltd., tel. 724−0421/4
The Mitsubishi Bank, Ltd, tel. 777−9561/4
The Mitsui Bank, Ltd, tel. 778−4631

Bank of Montreal, tel. 778−0631/4
Bank of Nova Scotia, tel. 778−0631
Royal Bank of Canada, tel. 776−7553
International Bank of Singapore,
tel. 778−3174
Hongkong and Shanghai Banking Corp,
tel. 22−9119

Korean

Bank of Korea, tel. 771−07
Bank of Seoul and Trust Co, tel. 771−60
Cho-Heung Bank, Ltd, tel. 724−0561
Citizens National Bank, tel. 771−40
Commercial Bank of Korea, Ltd,
tel. 771−30
Export-Import Bank of Korea,
tel. 778−3950
Hanil Bank, Ltd, tel. 771−20
Korea Development Bank, tel. 771−65
Korea Exchange Bank, tel. 771−46
Korea First Bank, Ltd, tel. 771−70

Hotels, Inns and Hostels

Since 1978, when over one million foreign visitors arrived in Korea, there has been a major boom in the Korean hotel industry. There are now 160 tourist hotels registered with the government; most include standard international facilities, such as restaurants and bars, coffee shops, recreational facilities, telecommunication services and other amenities.

Hotels in Korea are divided into four classes: Deluxe at US$65−115 for a twin with bath; First Class at US$50−75; Second Class at US$30−45 and Third Class at US$25−35.

Korean inns (*yogwan*) are a pleasant alternative to international hotels. Equipped with *ondol* (warm floor) heating systems, quilted bedding and other traditional touches, *yogwan* immerse your senses in classical Korean comforts. Rooms in good *yogwan* in Seoul run from US$15−25 per night — less down south. Most international hotels keep one or two floors of traditional style *yogwan* rooms, so you can try one for a night or two even in the Hilton or Sheraton.

For budget travellers, Korea has about two dozen youth hostels scattered across the peninsula. Single room rates range from US$5−10 per night.

For complete listings of recommended hotels and *yogwan*, pick up a copy of KNTC's Hotel Guide, or contact the Korea Tourist Association at 757−2345 in Seoul, or the Korea Hotel Central Association at 783−9866. For further information on hostels, contact the Korea Youth Hostel Association at 266−2896 in Seoul.

Hotels

Seoul

Seoul's 'Top Seven' hotels are listed first, followed by a selection of others in various classes:

Deluxe

Westin Chosun
87, Sokong-dong,
Chung-ku
CPO Box 3706
tel. 771−05, tx. 24256
cable WESTCHOSUN

471 rooms

Seoul's oldest international hotel, with excellent restaurants and bar, nightclub, shopping arcade, swimming pool; central location downtown, traditional decor.

Seoul Hilton International
395, 5-ka, Namdaemunno,
Chung-ku
tel. 753−7788

629 rooms

The newest of Seoul's top seven, with a spacious marble lobby and well-appointed rooms. Standard Hilton services and quality.

Lotte
1, Sogong-dong, Chung-ku
CPO Box 3500
tel. 771–10, tx. 28313
cable HOTELLOTTE

975 rooms

Central downtown location, largest hotel in Seoul. Thirty-one restaurants and bars, health club, indoor swimming pool, shopping arcade.

Seoul Plaza
23, 2-ka Taepyong-ro,
Chung-ku
tel. 771–22, tx. 26215
cable PLAZA HL SEOUL

542 rooms

Near Chosun and Lotte downtown.

Shilla
202, 2-ka, Changchung-dong, Chung-ku
tel. 233–3131, tx. 24160
cable HOTEL SHILLA

672 rooms

Located on a hill near Namsan; health club, swimming pool, disco and 23-acre garden.

Hyatt Regency
747–7, Hannam-dong,
Yongsan-ku
CPO Box 3438
tel. 798–0061, tx. 24136
cable HYATT SEOUL

604 rooms

Located on Mt Namsan, with great views of the city; outdoor pool, health club, disco, gourmet restaurant.

Sheraton Walker Hill
San 21, Kwangjang-dong,
Songdong-ku
tel. 453–0121, tx. 28517
cable WALKERHILL
SEOUL

770 rooms

Located on Walker Hill on 139 landscaped acres on outskirts of Seoul; indoor and outdoor pools, tennis, jogging trails; famous Kayagum Theatre Restaurant, plus Seoul's only licensed casino.

Ambassador Hotel
186–54, 2-ka,
Changchung-dong,
Chung-ku
CPO Box 1222
tel. 275–1101, tx. 23269
cable AMBASSADOR
SEOUL

451 rooms

Located at the foot of Namsan, next to the National Theatre.

King Sejong Hotel
61–3, 2-ka, Chungmu-ro,
Chung-ku
tel. 776–1811, tx. 27265
cable HOTESEJONG

250 rooms

Downtown near business and shopping districts below Mt Namsan.

Koreana Hotel
61–1, 1-ka, Taepyong-ro,
Chung-ku
tel. 730–8611, tx. 26241
cable HOTELKOREANA

271 rooms

Downtown near Kyongbok Palace and City Hall, near shopping districts.

President Hotel
188−3, 1-ka, Ulchi-ro,
Chung-ku
CPO Box 4569
tel. 753−2171, tx. 27521
cable HOTEL
PRESIDENT

303 rooms

Located in downtown city centre, across from City Hall.

Seoul Royal Hotel
6, 1-ka, Myong-dong
Chung-ku
tel. 771−45, tx. 27239
cable ROYALHOTEL

309 rooms

Located downtown near business and embassy districts.

First Class

Crown Hotel
34−69 Itaewon-dong,
Yongsan-ku
CPO Box 390
tel. 797−4111, tx. 25951

157 rooms

Located in Itaewon, near Yongsan Garrison.

Hamilton Hotel
119−25 Itaewon-dong,
Yongsan-ku
tel. 794−0171/9, tx. 24491

139 rooms

Located in Itaewon, near foot of Namsan.

New Kukje Hotel
29−2,1-ka, Taepyong-ro,
Chung-ku
tel. 732−0161, tx. 24760
cable NEW KUKTEL

149 rooms

Located in downtown business district.

New Seoul Hotel
29−1, 1-ka, Taepyong-ro,
Chung-ku
CPO Box 3385
tel. 735−9071, tx. 27220
cable SELOTEL

151 rooms

Near the downtown city centre.

Pacific Hotel
31−1, 2-ka, Namsan-dong,
Chung-ku
CPO Box 5975
tel. 777−7811, tx. 26249
cable HOTEL PACIFIC

103 rooms

Near downtown and Namsan Park.

Poongjun Hotel
73−1, 2-ka, Inhyon-dong,
Chung-ku
tel. 266−2151
cable HOTEL
POONGJUN

227 rooms

In the downtown city centre.

Seoulin Hotel
149, Sorin-dong, Chongro-
ku
tel. 732−0181, tx. 28510
cable HOTEL SEOULIN

Located in downtown city centre, near shopping and business districts.

Tower Hotel
San 5−5, 2-ka,
Changchung-dong,
Chung-ku
tel. 253−9181, tx. 28246
cable TOWERTEL

Atop Namsan, with panoramic views of Seoul.

Yoido Hotel
10−3, Yoido-dong,
Yongdungpo-ku
CPO Box 23
tel. 782−0121/5
cable YOIDHOTEL

On Youido Island, near National Assembly.

Second Class

Astoria Hotel
13−2, Namhak-dong,
Chung-ku
tel. 267−7111/8

80 rooms

Near downtown shopping districts.

Central Hotel
227−1, Changsa-dong,
Chongro-ku
tel. 265−4120
cable CENTRAL

88 rooms

Near downtown shopping districts.

Hotel Green Park
San 14, Ui-dong, Tobong-
ku
tel. 993−2171

92 rooms

Located in northern suburbs of Seoul, on slopes of scenic Mt Pukhan.

Metro Hotel
199−33, Ulchi-ro,
Chung-ku
tel. 776−8221, tx. 26486
cable METROHOTEL

83 rooms

Located downtown near business district.

New Oriental Hotel
10, 3-ka, Hoehyon-dong,
Chung-ku
tel. 753−0701
cable NEWORIENTALH

84 rooms

Located near the downtown districts.

Savoy Hotel
23−1, 1-ka, Chungmu-ro,
Chung-ku
CPO Box 291
tel. 776−2641, tx. 23222
cable SAVOY HOTEL

107 rooms

Located in downtown city centre.

Seoul Rex Hotel
65, 1-ka, Hoehyon-dong,
Chung-ku
CPO Box 7798
tel. 752−3191
cable HOTELREX

111 rooms

Near downtown business districts.

Third Class

YMCA Hotel
9, 2-ka, Chong-ro,
Chongro-ku
tel. 732−8291/8
cable HOTEL YMCA

80 rooms

Central downtown location, close to shopping and
business districts.

Pusan

Deluxe

Chosun Beach Hotel
737, Wooil-dong, Tongrae-
ku
PO Box 29
tel. 72−7411/20, tx. 3718
cable WESTCHOSUN
BUSAN

333 rooms

Located on sunny Haeundae Beach, north of the city.

Commodore Dynasty Hotel
743−80, Yongju-dong,
Chung-ku
PO Box 407
tel. 44−9101/7, tx. 3717
cable COMMODORE
BUSAN

325 rooms

Downtown Pusan, on scenic hillside.

Sorabol Hotel
37−1, 1-ka,
Taechong-dong, Chung-ku
PO Box 693
tel. 463−3511, tx. 3827
cable SOHOTEL

Downtown business district.

First Class

Pusan Hotel
12, 2-ka, Tongkwang-
dong, Chung-ku
tel. 23−4301/9, tx. 3657
cable BUSANHOTEL

289 rooms

Located in central business district.

Kukdong Hotel
1124, Chung-dong,
Tongrae-ku
tel. 72−0081/90, tx. 3758
cable HOTEL
KUKDONG BUSAN

108 rooms

Located in Haeundae Beach Resort.

Phoenix Hotel
8−1, 2-ka, Chungmu-
dong, Chung-ku
tel. 22−8061/9, tx. 3704

120 rooms

Downtown business district.

Second Class

Busan Royal Hotel
2−72, 2-ka, Kwangbok-
dong, Chung-ku
tel. 23−1051/9
cable ELEPHANTEL

121 rooms

Near Yongdusan Park and Pusan Tower.

Busan Tower Hotel
20, 3-ka, Tongkwang-
dong, Chung-ku
tel. 243−1001

108 rooms

Near Pusan Tower and Yongdusan Park.

Third Class

Paradise Beach Hotel
1408−5, Chung-dong,
Haeundae-ku
tel. 72−1461/8
cable HOTEL
HAEUNDAE

38 rooms

Located in the Haeundae Beach Resort.

Inchon

First Class

Olympus Casino Hotel
3−2, 1-ka, Hang-dong,
Chung-ku
CPO Box 359
tel. 762−5181, tx. 24894
cable OLYMPOTEL

189 rooms

Built on a hillside overlooking the Yellow Sea.

Suwon

Second Class

Brown Hotel
47, Kuchon-dong
tel. 7−4141

61 rooms

Located in downtown Suwon.

Songtan

Second Class

Songtan Hotel
274−190, Shinjang-dong
tel. 4−5101/5

71 rooms

Located in Songtan, with quick access to Korean Folk
Village.

Kangwon-do Province

This province occupies the northwest corner of Korea and includes spectacular Mt Sorak
Park, coastal Kangnung, Mt Odae Park and Dragon Valley Ski Resort.

First Class

New Sorak Hotel
106−1, Sorak-dong,
Sokcho-si
tel. 7−7131/50, tx. 24893
cable NEWSORAK
HOTEL

120 rooms

Located in Mt Sorak National Park.

Sorak Park Hotel
74−3, Sorak-dong,
Sokcho-si
tel. 7−7711/22

121 rooms

Located in Mt Sorak National Park.

Second Class

Chunchon Sejong Hotel
San 1, Pongui-dong
tel. 52−1191

52 rooms

Set on a scenic hillside in the provincial capital of
Chunchon.

**Dragon Valley Ski Resort
Hotel**
130, Hoegye-ri, Toam-
myon, Pyongchang-kun
tel. 2168
cable DRAVAL RESRT

70 rooms

Located in rugged ski mountains near scenic east coast of
Korea.

Third Class

Dong Hae Hotel
274−1, Kangmun-dong,
Kangnung-si
tel. 2−2181

86 rooms

Located on hillside overlooking East Sea at Kyongpodae
Beach Resort, Kangnung.

Mt Sorak Hotel
170, Sorak-dong, Sokcho-si
tel. 7−7101

59 rooms

Located in Mt Sorak National Park.

New Chunchon Hotel
30−1 Nakwon-dong
tel. 3−8285

50 rooms

Located in downtown Chunchon City.

Mt Songni

First Class

Songnisan Hotel
198, Sanae-ri, Naesongni-
Poun-kun
tel. 2091/8

160 rooms

Located in the village at the entrance to Mt Songni Park.

Chungchongnam-do Province

This province occupies the central western coast of Korea, and includes the mineral-spa town of Onyang, Chonan, Taejon, and Taechon Beach.

Deluxe

Dogo Hotel
180−1, Kigok-ri,
Togo-myon, Asan-kun
tel. 2−6031
cable DOGOHOTEL

130 rooms

Located at the famous hot spring spa of Togo, east of Onyang.

First Class

Jeil Hotel
228−6, Onchon-ri,
Onyang-up, Asan-kun
tel. 2−6111
cable ONYANG JEIL

93 rooms

Located in the famous hot spring spa of Onyang.

Joon Ang Hotel
318, Chung-dong, Tong-ku
tel. 253−8801

75 rooms

Located in downtown Taejon.

You Soung Hotel
480, Pongmyong-ri,
Yusong-up, Taedok-kun
tel. 822−0611
cable
YOUSUNGGHOTEL

200 rooms

Located in the hot spring spa town of Yusong, near Taejon.

Second Class

Onyang Admiral Hotel
242−10, Onchon-ri,
Onyang-up, Asan-kun
tel. 2−2141

67 rooms

Located at Onyang hot spring spa.

Kwangju

Second Class

Kwang Ju Hotel
20, 2-ka, Kumnam-ro
tel. 232−6231
cable HOTEL
GWANGJU

59 rooms

Located in central downtown Kwangju.

Yosu

Third Class

Yeosu Hotel
766, Konghwa-dong
tel. 62−3131

50 rooms

Located in downtown Yosu on the scenic Hallyo
Waterway.

Kyongju

Deluxe

Kolon Hotel
111−1, Ma-dong
CPO Box 21
tel. 2−9001/4, tx. 4469
cable KOLHTL

240 rooms

Located in an expansive landscaped garden, close to the
Pulguk Temple in historic Kyongju.

Kyongju Chosun Hotel
410, Sinpyong-dong
CPO Box 35
tel. 2−9601, tx. 4467
cable WESTCHOSUN
KYO

304 rooms

Located on the banks of Lake Pomun, 20 minutes east of
Kyongju town.

Kyongju Tokyu Hotel
410, Sinpyong-dong
CPO Box 6
tel. 2−9901/16, tx. 4328
cable KYONGJU TOKYU

303 rooms

Located on the banks of Lake Pomun, 20 minutes east of
Kyongju town.

First Class

Kyongju Hotel Shilla
700−1, Chinhyon-dong
tel. 2−3256/9, tx. 24160
cable HOTEL SHILLA

101 rooms

Near Pulguk Temple in Kyongju.

Bomun Lake Hotel
645, Sinpyong-dong,
tel. 2−7931/6

30 rooms

Located at Lake Pomun in Kyongju, as an annex to the
Kyongju Hotel School run by KNTC.

Taegu

First Class

Daegu Soo Sung Lakeside Hotel
0−888−2 Tusan-dong, Soo song-ku
tel. 763−7311

72 rooms

Located near the downtown and sightseeing districts of Taegu.

Dong In Hotel
5−2, 1-ka, Samdok-dong, Chung-ku
tel. 46−7211/9, tx. 4325

92 rooms

Located in central downtown Taegu.

Royal Hotel
24−4, Namil-dong, Chung-ku
tel. 253−5546
cable ROYAL HOTEL

50 rooms

Central downtown Taegu.

Masan, Ulsan and Pohang

First Class

Pohang Beach Hotel
311−2 Songdo-dong, Pohang
tel. 3−1401

60 rooms

Ulsan Grand Hotel
256−20, Songnam-dong
tel. 44−1501

125 rooms

Located in downtown Ulsan on coast north of Pusan.

Tae Wha Hotel
1406−6, Sinjyung-dong
P.O. Box 117
tel. 73−3301

103 rooms

Located along the Tae Wha River in downtown Ulsan.

Lotte Crystal Hotel
3−6, 4-ka, Masan-si
tel. 2−1112/9
cable MASAN CRYSTAL

121 rooms

Located in downtown Masan with views of the sea and countryside.

Chungmu

Second Class

Chung Mu Tourist Hotel
1, Tonam-dong
tel. 2−2091/5, tx. 3850

50 rooms

Located on scenic promontory overlooking Chungmu and the Hallyo Waterway.

Hillside Hotel
San 34—1, Okpo-ri,
Changsungpo-up,
Koje-gun,
Kyongsangnam-do
tel. 32—2932

96 rooms

Cheju Island

Deluxe

Cheju Grand
263, Youn-dong,
PO Box 45
tel. 42—3321, tx. 712
cable CHEJUGRANHTL

522 rooms

Situated in a quiet corner of New Cheju City.

Cheju KAL Hotel
1691—9, 2-do 1-dong,
PO Box 62,
tel. 53—6151
cable CHEJUKALHTEL

310 rooms

In downtown Cheju City.

Second Class

Paradise Jeju Hotel
1315, 2-do 1-dong
tel. 23—0171, tx. 728
cable PARADISE JEJU
HTL

57 rooms

Located in downtown Cheju City.

Sogwipo Park Hotel
674—1, Sokwi 3-ri, Sokwi-
up, Namcheju-jun,
tel. 62—2165, tx. 728
cable PARADISE JEJU
HTL

68 rooms

Located in Sogwipo, on southern shores of Cheju Island.

Seogwipo Lions Hotel
803, Sokwi 2-ri, Sokwi-up,
Namcheju-kun
tel. 62—4141/4

47 rooms

Located in Sogwipo, on southern shores of Cheju Island, with good views of the sea and Mt Halla.

Hyatt Regency
3039—1 Saektal-dong,
Sogwipo
tel. 32—2001

224 rooms

Youth Hostels

Seoul

Bando Youth Hostel
679−3 Yoksam-dong,
Kangnam-ku
tel. 567−3111

Academy House Youth Hostel
San 76, Suyu-dong,
Tobong-ku
tel. 993−6181

Pusan

Blue Bird Youth Hostel
42−1, Puyong-dong, So-ku
tel. 42−7630

Aerin Youth Hostel
1−41, Posu-dong,
Chung-ku
tel. 27−2222

Kumgang Youth Hostel
1−4 Onchon-dong,
Tongnae-ku
tel. 554−3235

Suwon

Suwon Youth Hostel
201−1, Kodung-dong,
Suwon
Tel. 5−3321 .

Kangwon-do Province (Mt Sorak)

Naksan Youth Hostel
30−1 Chonjin-ri
Kanghyon, Yangyang-kun
tel. 3416

Sorak Youth Hostel
170, Sorak-dong, Sokcho-si
tel. 7−7101

Puyo

Puyo Youth Hostel
105−1, Kukyo-ri, Puyo-up,
Puyo-kun
tel. 2−3101

Kyongju

Kyongju Youth Hostel
145−1, Kujong-dong,
Kyongju
tel. 2−9991

Kyongsangnam-do Province (Hallyo Waterway)

Koje-do Nong Jang Youth Hostel
Chisepo-ri, Hun-myon,
Koje-kun (Koje Island)

Aekwang Youth Hostel (Beachside)
Mt 4−8, Changsungpo-ri,
Koje-kun

Aekwang Youth Hostel (Mountainside)
Mt 110, Kuchon-ri,
Tongbu-myon, Koje-kun
tel. 2324, 2325

Masan Youth Hostel
Mt 48−3, Kyobang-dong,
Masan
tel. 2−8164

Korean Kisaeng Houses

The ultimate dining and cultural experience in Seoul — combining traditional food, drink and entertainment within the context of classical Korean culture — is an evening at a Korean *kisaeng* house, an experience which requires a considerable outlay of cash. Somewhat similar in style to Japan's *geisha* houses but far less stiff and formal, Korean *kisaeng* houses take your body and soul back to the graceful, pampered leisure life enjoyed by ancient Korea's privileged elite. The cost usually comes to about US$50–70 per person for food and drinks, plus another $30 or so in tips for the ladies who accompany guests through dinner.

Historically, *kisaeng* were the only women in Korea who received formal education and enjoyed at least a semblance of public life and personal freedom. Although their careers ended abruptly soon after the age of 30, during the flower of youth famous *kisaeng* ranked among the kingdom's most well-known and admired personalities, much as famous movie-stars are today.

Unless you happen to speak fluent Korean, it is always advisable to visit *kisaeng* houses in the company of at least one Korean acquaintance, otherwise you will miss all the fun and games. Your party will have a private dining room decorated entirely in classical Korean fashion, and you will be served by a bevy of attractive young *kisaeng* clad in colourful Korean dress, who will pour your drinks, serve your food, wipe your brow, and entertain you with their charm.

Should you happen to establish rapport with one of the girls during the evening and wish to invite her out later for further entertainment elsewhere, bear in mind that she is under no obligation to go out with you. But if she does, the fee for her company is bound to be high. This question should always be directed to your Korean friend, who will act as honourable intermediary and consult the house *mama-san*, who makes all decisions and sets all fees at a *kisaeng* house. On the other hand, if you are with a mixed group, do not hesitate to bring a spouse or date to a *kisaeng* party, because *kisaeng* houses cater with equal grace and hospitality to both mixed parties and all-male groups.

Seoul's best known *kisaeng* house is the Dai Won Gak, a beautiful walled garden-compound with individual dining pavilions, thatched cottages, and landscaped ponds all connected by wooded walkways. Accustomed to hosting foreign parties, the Dai Won Gak can handle groups of two to one hundred with equal ease. Another popular *kisaeng* house is the Jang Wong, located about 65 metres (200 feet) in front of the police box behind the American Embassy.

Restaurants

Some of the more popular restaurants in Seoul, Pusan, Kyongju and Cheju are listed below.

Seoul

Korean Restaurants

Contemporary Gourmet Style These restaurants offer gourmet Korean cuisine in relatively contemporary settings. Service is usually very efficient and fast, and prices are reasonable.

Sorabol (Gourmet Korean cuisine)
Shilla Hotel
tel. 233−3131

Posokjong (Bulgogi beef, hanjongshik)
Lotte Hotel
tel. 771−10

Eunhasu (Korean buffet, traditional music performance)
Sejong Hotel
tel. 776−1811

Naksan Garden (Kalbi beef)
1−36 Dongsung-dong, Chongru-ku
tel. 742−7470

Shinjong (Hot pot, Korean beef)
21, 2-ka, Myong-dong, Chung-ku
tel. 776−1464

Hanilkwan (Traditional Korean cuisine)
50−1, 2-ka, Myong-dong, Chung-ku
tel. 776−3388

Buil Barbecued Rib House
Ulchi-ro, Chung-ku
tel. 777−1666

Sanchon (Korean vegetarian cuisine)
22 Kwanhun-dong, Chongro-ku
tel. 735−0321

Teppanyaki Beef Style These restaurants specialize in beefsteak and Oriental vegetables cooked on a griddle at your table.

Flamenco Steak House
53−6, 2-ka, Myong-dong, Chung-ku
tel. 776−3378

Pine Hill
88−5 Da-dong, Chung-ku
tel. 266−4486

Jumbo Steak House
President Hotel
tel. 753−2171

Deluxe Traditional Style These restaurants specialize in Korean banquets served in traditional surroundings by hostesses dressed in Korean attire. Some of them are also *kisaeng* houses, and they tend to run a bit on the expensive side.

Daewongak
323, Seongpuk-dong, Seongpuk-ku
tel. 765−0161

Daeha
56, Igseon-dong, Chongru-ku
tel. 765−1151

Seonwoongak
260−6, Wooi-dong, Dobong-ku
tel. 989−3986

Korea House
80−2, Pil-dong, 2 -ka, Chung-ku
tel. 266−9101

Banjul (Continental and Oriental)
12–16, Gwanchul-dong, Chongru-ku
tel. 733–4432

La Cantina (Italian)
Samsung Building, 1–50, Eulji-ro
tel. 777–2579

Shangrila (Western and Oriental Buffet)
Shilla Hotel
tel. 233–3131

Plaza (Steaks and Seafood)
1–124, Youido-dong, Yongdungpo-ku
tel. 782–4171

Western Restaurants

The Ninth Gate (French)
Chosun Hotel
tel. 771–05

Prince Eugene (French)
Lotte Hotel
tel. 771–10

Celadon Restaurant (Continental)
Sheraton Walker Hill Hotel
tel. 453–0121

El Toro (American-style steaks)
Seoul Plaza Hotel
tel. 771–22

Chinese and Japanese Restaurants

Moon Palace (Northern Chinese)
Chosun Hotel, 20th Floor
tel. 771–05

Tao Yuen (Northern Chinese)
Seoul Plaza Hotel, 3rd Floor
tel. 771–22

Dongbosong (Chinese)
50–8 Namsan-dong, 2-ka, Chung-ku
tel. 755–2727

Palsun (Cantonese and Sichuanese)
Shilla Hotel, 2nd Floor
tel. 233–3131

Mandarin (Chinese)
640–2 Shinsa-dong, Kangnam-ku
tel. 542–3456

Ariake (Japanese)
Shilla Hotel, 2nd Floor
tel. 233–3131

Benkay (Japanese)
Lotte Hotel, lower arcade
tel. 771–10

Akasaka (Japanese)
Hyatt Hotel, lower arcade
tel. 798–0061

Food Street (Chinese, Japanese, and
Korean speciality restaurants)
Ninth and Tenth Floors
Lotte Shopping Centre

Dinner Theatres

Kayagum Dinner Theatre (With huge floor
shows, Las Vegas-style)
Sheraton Walker Hill
tel. 453–0121

Korea House (Traditional service or
buffet, classical performances)
80–2, Pil-dong, 2-ka, Chung-ku
tel. 266–9101

Pusan

Kaya (Korean)
15–4 Chungang-dong, 4-ka, Chung-ku
tel. 463–3277

Sorabol Kalbi (Korean)
1489–10, Chung 2-dong, Haeundae-ku
tel. 72–7675

Haeundae Jib (Korean)
1228, Chung 1-dong, Haeundae-ku
tel. 72–1609

Ninth Gate (European)
Westin Chosun Beach Hotel
tel. 72–7411

Chung Tap Grill (Western)
36, Nampo-dong, 2-ka, Chung-ku
tel. 23–0071

Dabotap (Western)
Hotel Sorabol
tel. 463–3511

Kuk Je (Northern Chinese)
Pusan Commodore Hotel
tel. 44–9107

Kuromatsu (Japanese)
Westin Chosun Beach Hotel
tel. 72–7411

Suck Tap (Japanese)
193–1, Kwangan 2-dong, Nam-ku
tel. 753–0010

Kyongju

Geo Goo Jang (Korean, Japanese)
220, Shinpyong-dong
tel. 2–8624

Hobajang (Korean, with classical music
and dance performance)
410, Shinpyong-dong
tel. 2–9901

Kyongju Kalbi (Korean kalbi, bulgogi
beef)
749 Inwang-dong
tel. 2–5262

Sorabol (Korean)
Kyongju Chosun Hotel
tel. 2–9601

Ninth Gate (European)
Kyongju Chosun Hotel
tel. 2–9601

King's Arms (Western)
Kyongju Tokyu Hotel
tel. 2–9901

Lotus (Japanese)
Kyongju Kolon Hotel
tel. 2–9001

Cheju

Haewon (Korean)
Hyatt Regency Hotel
tel. 32–2001

Samdajung (Korean)
Cheju Grand Hotel
tel. 42–3321

Azalea (Western)
Cheju Grand Hotel
tel. 42–3321

Fontainbleau (European)
Cheju Grand Hotel
tel. 42–3321

Dagmar's (Western)
Hyatt Regency Hotel
tel. 32–2001

Umbibe (Japanese)
Hyatt Regency Hotel
tel. 32–2001

Holidays and Festivals

National Holidays

1 January, New Year's Day
The first three days of January are officially recognized as the beginning of the New Year and are celebrated as national holidays. Most Koreans, however, still celebrate the Lunar New Year, which falls in late January or early February.

1 March, Independence Day (Samil-jol)
Samil, which means 'three/one' (third month, first day) celebrates the anniversary of the 1 March 1919 Independence Movement against Japan's colonial occupation of Korea. On this day, the Declaration of Independence signed by 33 Korean patriots in 1919 is read publicly at Pagoda Park in Seoul.

5 April, Arbor Day
This holiday is observed by both children and adults, who fan out in festive groups throughout the country to plant trees, shrubs, and flowers.

Buddha's Birthday (eighth day of fourth lunar month, usually early-May)
Declared a national holiday in 1975, the Festival of the Lanterns marks the birth of Sakyamuni Buddha 2,500 years ago. Wherever you happen to be in Korea on this day, try to spend it in a Buddhist temple — especially towards early evening, when hundreds of colourful lanterns are lit by the faithful. In Seoul, the Chogye Temple is the most popular place to celebrate Buddha's Birthday and enjoy the festivities.

5 May, Children's Day
Originally celebrated as Boys' Day, Children's Day was declared a Korean national holiday in 1975 in order to further forge the all-important bonds of family life in Korea.

6 June, Memorial Day
On this solemn occasion, Koreans pay formal tribute to those who gave their lives fighting for their country. In Seoul, this day is observed with memorial services at the National Cemetery.

15 June, Farmers' Day
This day is a time for all Koreans to remember that 'every grain of rice represents a drop of sweat in the fields'. Though not a legal holiday, it is nevertheless observed with folk dances and traditional music at farmers' festivals in the provinces.

17 July, Constitution Day
This is a national holiday which commemorates the proclamation of the Constitution of the Republic of Korea on 17 July 1948. The occasion is marked with patriotic ceremonies in Seoul's capital plaza.

15 August, Liberation Day
Liberation Day celebrates the surrender of Japan to the Allies in 1945, and also marks the establishment of the Republic of Korea in 1948.

Chusok (15th day of eighth lunar month, usually mid-September)
Chusok is one of Korea's most ancient celebrations. Known as the 'Mid-Autumn Moon Festival' in China, Chusok is often referred to as 'Korean Thanksgiving'. The culmination of Chusok occurs when everyone proceeds to hills or lakeside pavilions to watch the rise of the biggest moon of the year — the 'Harvest Moon'.

1 October, Armed Forces Day
This holiday is held in honour of Korea's national defence forces and is marked by military parades, honour-guard ceremonies, air force aerial acrobatics and other military pageantry. Major ceremonies take place at the reviewing plaza on Yoi Island in the Han River southwest of Seoul.

3 October, National Foundation Day
Also known as Tangun Day, this holiday commemorates the founding of Korea by the legendary Tangun, Korea's first king, who is said to have established the nation in 2333 BC. The occasion is marked by ceremonies at the 'Altar of Tangun' on the summit of Mt Mani on Kanghwa Island.

9 October, Hangul Day
This holiday commemorates the invention and promulgation of *hangul*, Korea's indigenous alphabet, by King Sejong (reigned 1418–50).

24 October, United Nations Day
This is a solemn occasion, during which the UN soldiers who gave their lives in defence of South Korea during the Korean War are commemorated with memorial services at the UN Cemetery in Pusan, as well as in Seoul.

25 December, Christmas Day
Christmas Day is observed as a national holiday throughout Korea.

Annual Festivals

Tongshin-Je (15th day of first lunar month, usually mid-February)
An ancient festival related to Lunar New Year and shaman fertility rites, this is seldom observed today except in remote rural areas.

Unsan Village Ritual, April
Held annually at a shrine in a forest southwest of Unsan Village in Chungchongnam-do Province, this festival is celebrated for 12 days with ritual ceremonies, colourful processions and farmers' bands. It is held in honour of the mountain spirit and heroic generals.

Hanshik (105th day of lunar calendar)
Hanshik means 'cold food', and in ancient times people were not
supposed to build fires on this day. It is more commonly known to
Koreans and Chinese as 'Grave-Sweeping Day', and families observe
it by bringing food and wine to the gravesites of their ancestors.

**Chunhyang Festival (eighth day of fourth lunar month, usually early-
May)**
Falling on the same day as Buddha's Birthday, this festival is held at
Namwon town in Chollapuk-do Province in honour of Chunhyang, who
personifies the Confucian virtue of female fidelity.

Arang Festival, 9 May
Held at Milyang village in Kyongsangnam-do Province, this festival
commemorates the conjugal fidelity of Arang, a popular heroine of the
Silla Dynasty. Among the festivities is an interesting 'Miss Arang
Contest', which is held at Arang's memorial shrine. Contenders for the
title must demonstrate their virtuosity in the traditional arts of literary
composition, classical music, calligraphy and embroidery.

Tano Spring Festival (fifth day of fifth lunar month, early-June)
Tano Day is one of the three major festivals on the lunar calendar in
Korea, and is associated with ancient agricultural traditions. Originally
an occasion to pray for good harvests, Tano Day now includes other
festivities such as shaman rites, ancestor worship and folk music. This
festival continues for a full week at the eastern coastal town of
Kangnung.

Mahan Folk Festival, 8 October
A local festival held in the area of Iksan village in Chollapuk-do
Province, Mahan celebrates historical events and legends surrounding
the rise and fall of the Paekche Kingdom.

Andong Folk Festival, 28 September
Celebrated in Andong, this festival marks Confucius' birthday. It
features the Chajon-Nori (War of Dragons), during which two warriors
mounted on enormous A-frames manned by hundreds of people battle
to throw each other from their precarious perches.

Silla Cultural Festival, 8−10 October
One of the most colourful, exuberant festivals in Korea, this celebrates
the achievements of the Silla Dynasty. It is held in Kyongju and at
historical sites throughout the Kyongju Valley. Among the many events
are concerts, wrestling matches, Buddhist pagoda dancing, various
contests, and much more. Foreign tourists should try to witness this
festival if they happen to be in Korea when it occurs, but be sure to
make hotel or inn reservations in advance.

Chilsok (seventh day of seventh lunar month, usually mid-August)
According to ancient legends, the two stars known as the Herdboy
(Aquila) and the Weaving Girl (Vega), separated by the Milky Way,
meet only once a year on the seventh day of the seventh month of the
lunar calendar — the day these stars appear closest together in the sky.
It is a festival for young lovers and unmarried girls.

Paekche Cultural Festival, 13 October
The Paekche Cultural Festival takes place in Puyo and Kongju, former
capitals of the ancient Paekche Kingdom.

Moyang Castle Festival (ninth day of ninth lunar month, mid-October)
Moyang Castle was constructed in 1453, entirely by the labour of women
and girls. Held at Kochang town in Chollapuk-do Province, the festival
includes a procession of 5,000 women and girls, who parade along the
castle walls dressed in colourful costumes.

Halla Cultural Festival, 18−20 October
Celebrating Cheju Island's cultural legacy, this festival begins each year
with the ringing of every bell in every church and temple on the island
and the blasting of every steam-whistle on every boat in the harbour.

**Kaechon (National Foundation) Arts Festival (third day of tenth lunar
month, mid-November)**
This is held at Chinju in in recognition of that town's extensive cultural
contributions. Contests and exhibits of classical calligraphy and painting,
Chinese poetry, music and drama are included in a festival orchestrated
by scholars and students.

Recommended Reading

History

Deuchier, Martina. *Confucian Gentlemen and Barbarian Envoys* (Seoul: Royal Asiatic Society, 1977)

Han Woo-keun; trans, Lee Kyong-si. *History of Korea* (Honolulu: University of Hawaii Press, 1970)

Ledyard, Gari. *The Dutch Come to Korea* (1665, reprinted by Royal Asiatic Society and Taewon Publishing Co, 1971)

Culture and Society

Choe San-su. *Annual Customs of Korea* (Korea Book Publishing Co, 1960)

Covell, Jon Carter. *Korea's Cultural Roots* (Seoul: Hollym Publishers, third enlarged edition 1982)

Crane, Paul. *Korean Patterns* (Seoul: Royal Asiatic Society, 1967)

Gale, James S. *Korean Sketches* (1898, reprinted in Seoul by Royal Asiatic Society, 1975)

Kim Che-won, Kim Won-yong. *The Arts of Korea* (Charles E Tuttle, 1966)

Kim Yong-jong, ed. *Women of Korea — An History from Ancient Times to 1945* (Ewha Woman's University Press, 1976)

Lee Hye-gu. *An Introduction to Korean Music and Dance* (Royal Asiatic Society, 1977)

Lee, Peter H. *The traditional Culture and Society of Korea: Art and Literature* (Honolulu: University of Hawaii Press, 1975)

Lee Sun-ju. *Korean Folk Medicine* (Seoul: Publishing Centre of Seoul National University, 1966)

Osgood, Cornelius. *The Koreans and Their Culture* (Charles E Tuttle, 1964)

Religion

Clark, Charles Allan. *Religions of Old Korea* (1921, reprinted by Christian Literary Society of Korea, 1961)

Rutt, Richard. *Korean Works and Days: Notes From the Diary of a Country Priest* (Taewon Publishing Co, 1973)

Zozayong. *Korean Temple Paintings, Depicting the Life of Buddha* (Seoul: Royal Asiatic Society and Emille Museum, 1975)

Language and Literature

Ha Tae Hung. *Poetry and Music of the Classic Age* (Yonsei University Press, 1960)

Lee, Peter H. *Korean Literary History* (American Council of Learned Societies, 1963)

McCann, David R. *An Anthology of Korean Literature* (New York: Ithaca, Cornell University, 1977)

Rutt, Richard, ed. and trans. *The Bamboo Grove: An Introduction to Sijo* (poetry) (Berkeley: University of California Press, 1971)

Sohn Ho-min. *The Korean Language: Its Structure and Social Projection* (1975)

Zong In-sob. *Folk Tales From Korea* (Hollym Publishers, 1970)

Cuisine

Hyun, Judy. *The Korean Cookbook* (Hollym Publishers, 1970)

Mattielli, Sandra, and Rutt, Joan. *Lee Wade's Korean Cookbook* (Pomso Publishers, 1974)

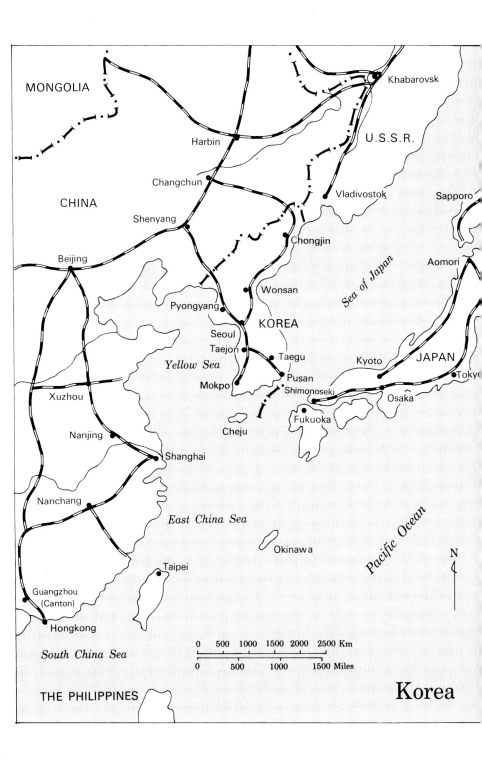

Index of Places